The
LAKE WASHINGTON
STORY

Aerial view over Bryn Mawr. The peninsula known as Pritchard Island is in the bay left. Beyond it Seward Park sticks a dark finger into the lake. *Photo by Greg Gilbert.*

The LAKE WASHINGTON STORY

A Pictorial History
By Lucile McDonald

Library of Congress Cataloging in Publication Data

McDonald, Lucile Saunders, 1898-
The Lake Washington story.

Bibliography: p.
Includes index.
SUMMARY: A physical and social history of Lake Washington, the 20-mile long body of water that forms the greater part of the eastern boundary of Seattle.
1. Washington, Lake, region, Wash.—History. 2. Washington, Lake, region, Wash.—Description and travel. [1. Washington, Lake, region, Wash.—History. 2. Washington, Lake, region, Wash.—Description and travel] i. Title.
F897.K4M3 979.7'77 7920102
ISBN 0-87564-635-2

FIRST EDITION

Photographic reproduction by Artcraft Colorgraphics—Seattle, WA.

Printed and bound in the United States of America

Contents

Articles which I wrote for The Seattle Times Sunday Magazine were the inspiration for this book and the source of some of the illustrations. Most of them were researched when a dozen or more well-informed early residents were still living and I was able to interview them. Other information was made available through diaries, letters and scrapbooks owned by descendants. As for libraries, I am indebted to the Northwest Collection, the Newspaper Division and the Law Library at the University of Washington, Seattle Public Library, and the Kirkland Public Library. Some of the pictures within were collected by me so long ago that I regret being unable to credit the sources. (Dust jacket photo by Josef Scaylea)

Lucile McDonald

The mountain as seen above Mercer Island and the Evergreen Point Bridge. *Photo by Greg Gilbert.*

Introducing the Lake

When one lives within sight of Lake Washington he accepts beauty as 24-hour fare, a treat outside the windows whatever the season or the hour of the day. Neither rain squalls nor misty fogs nor lashing winds can utterly diminish the grandeur of the scene.

Most of the time the view is placid, with ducks feeding along the shore, flowering trees and bushes struggling into bloom, pleasure boats scudding by, lush sunrises and sunsets, jewelled lights garlanding the distant hills, leafless branches framing views. There's always something to look at—light reflected on the water in a fresh pattern, a flock of geese flying overhead, waves from passing boats breaking against the banks, a bright blue sail rounding a point, a tugboat put-putting by with a tow of gravel barges.

The lake is very much a part of Seattle, for the 20-mile long body of water forms most of the city's eastern boundary. Because of it, boating, water-skiing and swimming are natural adjuncts of life.

Rare is the metropolitan area with such an asset. The city's growth has shown a tendency to take in as much of the shore as possible, so that Seattle's boundaries extend to Bryn Mawr on the south and almost to Sheridan Beach on the north. The remainder of the shoreline consists of heavily populated suburbs, linked by highways and two floating bridges—with more contemplated.

In spite of being surrounded by highly urbanized districts, the lake is big enough so that it creates a feeling of vast open spaces. On clear days one sees across it to two ranges of mountains. On the horizon there are always serrated tops of fir trees and during

View of Lake Washington looking east from Student Union Building, U. of W. *Photo by Greg Gilbert.*

most of the year the lighter green of cottonwoods. Weekends the water is dotted with sailboats.

Eighty-five years ago much of what one sees was a wilderness, with loggers beginning to leave their mark on the upland slopes. In 1850 it was Indian country, completely unknown to whites.

Lake Washington was the site of a glacier possibly 30,000 or 40,000 years ago. The last great invasion of ice, pushing from British Columbia through Washington as far south as Tenino, was squeezed between the Olympic and Cascade Ranges, conforming to the shape of Puget Sound. Ice a few thousand feet thick completely filled the Sound, Lake Washington, Lake Union and Lake Sammamish and covered the Seattle hills. It scooped out valleys and sculptured ridges and when it moved back to the north it left a series of fresh-water lakes.

The largest of these is Lake Washington, with a total area of 34.3 square miles, exclusive of Union Bay. With the bay it is 34.9 square miles. The lake is long and narrow, measuring 3.9 miles across at Leschi, its widest place, and averaging 2.5 miles width most of its course.

The deepest place is 221 feet near Madison Park. Much of the lake is approximately 200 feet deep. The University of Washington Oceanography Department, in charting the bottom, found it was carved originally to a depth of 350 feet. Sediment since has piled up to thicknesses as great as 150 feet in the deeper chasms. It is believed the first 100 feet of sediment was deposited soon after glaciers formed the basin and the last six inches in the 60 years since the ship canal was completed.

Because fossil shells have been found as much as 675 feet above present sea level, it is theorized that the whole valley south of Lake Washington must have been flooded by the ocean. Sea level dropped to the present point either because the land rose after the weight of ice was removed or it was pushed up by volcanic force.

However, investigations of recent years have demonstrated that the lake never was a part of the sea. All the mollusks brought up were fresh-water species.

The total shoreline of Lake Washington, excluding Mercer Island and Union Bay, is 53.2 miles. Figures related to the length vary. By air line and by navigable channel they disagree by two miles. Air-line length is 18 miles; by mid-channel it is 20.

Knowledge of the lake was vague at first and the 1869 Pacific Coast Pilot approached the subject cautiously, stating: "Lake Washington is reported to be 25 miles long and two or three miles wide, with islands in it."

By now this body of water has been studied repeatedly by geographers and scientists and there are few secrets left in its depths.

Black River as shown in an old photo.

Until fairly recent times the outlet was at the south end, through the now non-existent Black River. One can see traces of the old stream course in a depression south of the Boeing plant at Renton, a few feet to the east of Rainier Avenue.

Before man altered the flow of streams in that sector, the Cedar River was not one of its main tributaries and did not pour directly into the lake, but ran across the lower portion of what is now the Renton airport and drained into the Black River. Together they flowed into the Duwamish River. Thus the present mouth of the Cedar River is an artificial one, contained in a canal through the Boeing property.

The shores had a very different appearance in some places when there was more water in the lake and it was approximately nine feet higher than at present. Gardens of some homes along the shore reveal the old beach level as a terrace. Sloping lawns all around the lake have an underlying deposit of fine sand, a heritage from the days when the water was only a few feet away.

Today the elevation of the lake is 14½ feet above mean sea level. Instead of being higher than Lake Union, as formerly, the two bodies have been equalized by the flow through the ship canal.

Scientists have explored the bottom of Lake Washington and ascertained by means of soundings that it has a W-shaped hump on the bottom, believed to have been formed by cold water plunging downward near the shores and piling the sediment in a central ridge. Geologists call this the convection process.

The bottom of the lake is floored with blue clay, the sedimentary rock flour left by melting glaciers. Over this is a layer of compact white volcanic ash, deposited approximately 12,000 years ago by the great eruption of Glacier Peak in the primitive region north of Stevens Pass. On top of this souvenir of the era of lava flows are 20 feet of diatomaceous sediment, the remains of small planktonic organisms which are the main type living in the lake today.

Between layers of peat is to be found the residue of still another volcanic upheaval, ash from Mount Mazama (Crater Lake) in Southern Oregon, which erupted 6,000 years ago. Thus, cores taken from the lake bottom contain an entire geologic record of what went on in the Pacific Northwest in past ages.

Sunken Forests

The lake has three sunken forests caused by landslides, which may have resulted from saturation of the steep slopes as the level of the water rose. A wave-cut bench, 40 feet below the surface, may have been the lowest level. The water rose when the delta of the Cedar River was built up.

Tree brought up from the sunken forest by a University of Washington geology group. *Seattle Times photo.*

The W.T. Preston, venerable snag boat of the Department of the Army, Seattle District Corps of Engineers, at work on Lake Washington. *Photo courtesy U.S. Engineers*

One of the sunken forests has been dated by pulling up a tree from the bottom and subjecting a sample to the Carbon 14 process. It was a Douglas fir, still sound inside after 1,100 years of immersion.

It is believed that when this sunken forest slid more than a millenium ago the lake was 12 to 20 feet lower than now.

One sunken forest is north of Denny Park, another is opposite Mercer Heights and the third is at the south end of Mercer Island. When discovered by wire-dragging these were whole groves of trees standing upright on plateaus 100 feet below the surface of the water. It used to be said that this was the only place in the United States where a ship could be hung up in tree tops. They were blasted off or pulled out to a depth of 12 or more feet below the surface by the U.S. Engineers Corps snagboat in 1917, so as not to endanger navigation.

The present government snagboat, a venerable sternwheeler, the *W.T. Preston*, still operates on the lake, although she covers other tributaries of Puget Sound as well. The steel vessel was built in 1939 especially for this work. The engines and some of the equipment were transferred from her predecessor. Though 163 feet long, the *Preston* draws little more than three feet of water and can work close to shore. She carries a 7-foot boom and an assortment of cables, chokers, winches and tongs, calculated to grapple with deadheads, floating debris and sunken boats.

A holding area for such waste, near the west end of the Evergreen Point Bridge, is used by both the *Preston* and a scow owned by Seattle's Engineering Department. Here rubbish accumulates inside a boom and when there is enough for a bargeload it is removed to a disposal site on the Tulalip Indian Reservation near Everett.

Indians Always Had a Name for It

Before white men mapped the Pacific Northwest the Indians had their names for landmarks which tell a little about the red men's association with Lake Washington, which they called It-how-chug, large lake. One name indicated that a sizeable fish trap made of piling stood in Union Bay where the water from Green Lake, flowing down a stream winding through present Ravenna Park, emptied into the large body of water.

Near Bryn Mawr was an old village site called the "Place Where One Wades" and at the mouth of a creek north of Rainier Beach was "Loon," for the birds which nested in the nearby swamp. "Paint" was Nelson Point, on the south side of Juanita Bay, where coloring matter was scraped from the rocks, baked in a campfire and became face paint.

"Small Rushes for Mats" was south of Leschi Park and "Where One Chops" was Madison Park. East Seattle on Mercer Island was "The Place Where Gooseberry Bushes Grow." May Creek, on the east side near Kennydale, was "The Place Where Things Are Dried," for the drying of redfish—that is, salmon.

Sheridan Beach was "Thunderbird House," so it may be no coincidence that an apartment building there is named Thundalarra. The mythical bird which could cause storms by clapping its wings and winking its eyes was believed to nest on a bluff in that vicinity.

Sheridan Beach was Thunderbird House to the Indians. The big bird lived on the bluff. *Photo by Greg Gilbert.*

Brighton Beach was "Forbidden Place," where another supernatural creature lived. The south point of Mercer Island was "Stripping," because of a legendary old man who went there by canoe to gather bark from dead trees. Earth beings lived in the old stumps and when he removed the bark it was like taking away their clothing, so went the tale. The creatures drove the old man crazy and for that reason the Indians feared the place.

Foster Island was "Tiny Island," where the trees were full of burial boxes. The portage between the lakes was "Where One Lifts His Canoe."

Most amusing of the Indian names was that given to the lake shore at Kenmore—Sta tabeb, meaning "Lots of People Talking."

Isaac N. Ebey, who was the first white man to visit Lake Washington. *Seattle Times photo.*

Foster Island was once an Indian burial place. *Photo by Greg Gilbert.*

Coming of the White Men

When the first white men appeared in the country they had no knowledge of the lake until a young lawyer, Isaac N. Ebey, shortly after his arrival in Washington Territory in the summer of 1850, went looking for land. He left Olympia in a canoe to seek suitable farm sites for himself and his relatives. First he examined the mouth of the Puyallup River, decided to pass it by and went on to what he called the Dewams, the present Duwamish. Here he turned into the meandering stream and noted much rich bottom soil. He continued inland and related that 20 miles upstream the river forked, one branch having its source in a large clear lake surrounded by heavy forests of cedar, fir, maple, ash and oak.

"I traveled on it to the north a distance of more than 20 miles," he guessed, "without finding its terminus. The water is clear and very deep; from the beauty of the lake we christened it by the name of Geneva.* Another lake of less extent lies about two miles to the east of Geneva and is connected with it by a small stream."

Ebey said that between the lake and Admiralty Inlet appeared to be an extensive lowland that had never been examined by white men. The distance between the lake and salt water, he was certain, in many places could not exceed a few miles, as the Indians reported portaging across it with their canoes.

Several settlers soon took land claims in the Duwamish Valley. Ebey, however, was not among them. He went on to Whidbey Island and made his home there.**

The next chapter of lake history was during the Indian War. The lake was on the route from Eastern Washington to Puget Sound by way of Cedar River and the mountain pass at its head. In January, 1856 hostile tribesmen crossed Lake Washington, descended by forest trails upon the tiny settlement of Seattle, made a quick attack and retreated to the tall timber. The soldiers pursuing them went up the Duwamish River, where there also had been assaults on the settlers, and endeavored to flush out Indians along the lake shore. Some of the troops entered Black River in canoes in a pouring rain, marched through the woods in the night and arrived at a site where about 400 Indians had camped at the edge of a swamp.

**Note:* In 1863 the lake was still on government maps as Dawamish or Dwamish.

***Note:* Since Ebey was the first white man who claimed to have seen Lake Washington, we should add that Mrs. David Maynard said she was the first white woman to view it, when in 1853, the year she was married, she accompanied her husband up the Duwamish and Black Rivers by canoe.

Looking upstream on the Duwamish River above Allentown.

Although the tribesmen were gone, Captain Edward Lander reported, "Here we found wheat, fish and ox bones, showing clearly that to this place the Indians who attacked Seattle and burned the houses on the Duwamish River retreated to enjoy their plunder."

He believed his expedition had driven the dangerous Indians from this part of Seattle's hinterland. The volunteer troops scoured the western shore of the lake from Black River to the favorite portage to the Sound by way of Montlake, Lake Union and Salmon Bay. Lander mentioned that one detachment had been sent 16 miles through the forest from Georgetown to the Montlake portage. This same spot was one day to become part of the Lake Washington Ship Canal. Within a few years it was heavily traveled by Indians en route to pick the white farmers' hops in the valleys to the south and east.

Although the shore of the lake was by now somewhat known, it was still a long way from attracting settlers. Scattered land claims were taken on both sides of the winding Duwamish River as far as Renton, but Lake Washington remained deserted by all except Indians until a flurry was created by discoveries of coal, which in that era was the all-important treasure men were seeking. It brought ships and industries, and Seattle was in need of both.

Coal mining in the early period. *Seattle Historical Society.*

Discovery of the Coal Fields

Existence of coal at Renton became known when Seattle was a tiny cluster of houses and the total white population of King County was only 154 persons.

Dr. R.H. Bigelow is credited with finding the black mineral in August, 1853 while clearing land near the head of navigation on the Duwamish River. Exactly where this was is not known, but one historian placed the first mine beyond the south end of Williams Street, approximately in Renton's Talbot district. An old map indicates that a coal outcropping was worked on the Christian C. Clymer mine on the west bank of the river.

Clymer, Henry H. Tobin, Joseph Fanjoy and O.M. Eaton were among the donation land claim seekers who went that year toward the head of the Duwamish, looking for the 320 and 640-acre tracts the government would allow them to prove up on. This group found what they were seeking near the junction of the Black and Cedar Rivers where, in February, 1854, they jointly launched a sawmill having two circular saws. Before that Fanjoy and Eaton helped Bigelow open his coal deposit. It was mined in a small way until the Indian war put an end to Bigelow's activities.

Meanwhile the sawmill, the first in King County outside of Seattle, made its mark in history. A contemporary newspaper account described it as being "above Duwamish Falls . . . one of the most desirable and valuable locations on the Sound." It was near the present main highway intersection on the west side of Renton, where the Black and Cedar poured their mingled waters into the Duwamish. A dam was required for power to drive the equipment and when the partners placed the initial timbers for this barrier across Black River the current reversed and seemed to flow back into the lake.

Fearing that the dam might raise the level of Lake Washington and cause it to flow out at some other low spot and defeat their purpose, Eaton offered to carry on more intensive exploration of the almost unknown body of water. He went with several Indians in a canoe and after several days returned to reassure his associates that the shore was watertight and they had nothing to be apprehensive about.

The completed dam was only six feet high but it was six weeks before the water raised sufficiently to pass over it.

The mill's career ended soon because no road reached it and the river, through which the partners had to transport their lumber, was extremely winding. Eaton and Fanjoy were murdered by Indians before proving up on their donation claims and the tribesmen, disgruntled at the failure of their attack on Seattle, burned the mill. Tobin died and his widow married Erasmus Smithers, her next door neighbor to the south. This was good fortune for her. Smithers later (in 1870) found a workable coal deposit on his land and because of it Renton began to grow.

Despite Bigelow's discovery, real interest in coal beds was not aroused until L.H. Andrews carried a flour sack filled with the black fuel from Issaquah in the fall of 1862 to a Seattle gunsmith who owned a small foundry. The latter sent a five-ton scow with sweeps and sail up the Duwamish and into the two lakes to fetch a load to be tested in his furnace. The scow, manned by Indians, required 20 days to make the round trip and traveled 140 miles. Part of the way it was poled over sand bars in the Duwamish by men walking from bow to stern as they pushed their poles in the soft mud.

The following year more coal was located by Edwin Richardson while he was surveying a township. The deposit was on the north bank of Coal Creek, less than three miles inland from Lake Washington. Prospectors hastened to file preemption claims on the mineral belt in the range of hills between the two lakes, among them some of Seattle's leading pioneers. They organized companies, particularly the Lake Washington Coal Co. in 1866 at what was later known as Newcastle. One of its founders was the Rev. George Whitworth, who had lived in Eastern mining regions and came to Seattle as a missionary, organizing the first Presbyterian church in the city. His associates were the Rev. Daniel Bagley, P.H. Lewis, John Ross and Selucius Garfielde, Olympic Peninsula politician.

A tunnel was opened near Coal Creek and very crude excavation was done at first. The vein was said to be seven feet thick. A rough wharf was constructed on the lakeshore and the coal was brought there over a dirt road.

A diary kept by Ross in February, 1867 gives an idea of the initial work getting ready to remove the coal. He spoke of cutting down trees, putting logs in the creek and preparing a road bed. He went to Seattle to fetch 25 pounds of pork and a sack of salt. On returning to the lakeshore he found the canoe in which he had traveled was split, so he and a man had to repair it, using tacks and 59 cents worth of tin. He worked on the road again, did some surveying and saw a bear, then quarried stone for several days to be used on the route. He went again to town for a sack of flour. After that he labored on the road until snow fell, five inches deep and this stopped construction nearly a month. When he went back there was still snow and he caught a cold and had to go home. Once more he carried provisions to the mine in April, then went to work intermittently quarrying rock, laying corduroy and doing other road chores. The wharf was built in May and by June Ross was wheeling coal.

The company acquired a 54-foot barge and Whitworth's son, James Edwin, poled and sailed it for a time. On its first trip it grounded in the Duwamish and when the coal finally reached its destination customs officers seized the craft for operating in salt water without a license and fined the owners $50.

Young Whitworth also was a diary keeper and in 1869 he jotted details of his round trips, which generally took five days. Among his entries about the upbound journey he wrote:

"We got two Indians and got up to Mr. Clymer's at noon. Got up to Black River for dinner. Got up to the fish trap (operated by Indians) and stayed all night . . . Hauled up to Smithers' barn and landed his feed . . . Took on hay at Cedar River, ran on a log at Smithers' barn and layed all night. Got supper at Smithers'."

On another occasion young Whitworth was thankful the scow was maneuvered through Black River without requiring the help of Indians. It often grounded on the flats and remained there until a change of tide. Another time he observed, "Had a rough job getting through Black River." That same trip he said, "We got up to the wharf, got loaded and got back as far as Cedar River bridge." The scow remained there overnight and next day he continued, "We was on Cedar River bar till after noon." Before he reached Seattle he was on two or three more bars, not getting through Black River until 9 a.m. the following day.

It is difficult to picture the problems of the Black River passage since the stream has almost completely vanished. Above the junction, where Cedar River poured into it, lay the lip of Lake Washington, a shallow place which presented an obstacle to anything larger than a canoe. But the passage had to be negotiated, for there were no roads and this was the only way the coal could be brought out.

The Homestead Period

While the coal mining industry was in its infancy the remainder of the lake country slowly came to life. Indians still lived around, but except at Renton, their retreats were scattered rather than in villages. They had favorite gathering places where salmon were running, on the Cedar River, where they constructed a weir, and at the mouth of the Sammamish. Leschi was a pull-up beach for their canoes, as yet the only craft available for travel. Except for coal barges, these were the only means of transportation in 1870 when men were combing the forests in search of free land.

They had been coming in since the beginning of Seattle, spreading out in search of big tracts. A homestead was no longer a great donation claim, but a quarter section, 160 acres, or only half that amount in areas where railroads had been granted lands. Gradually the contours of the region became known as men, by ones and twos and threes, explored the Indian trails. A venturesome fellow as early as 1848 had been to Snoqualmie Falls, finding his way up the Snoqualmie River with an Indian guide. Ten years later two settlers located on the prairie above the falls and in another four years the first comers were at Issaquah.

Events on Lake Sammamish were inseparably bound to those on Lake Washington, for the two bodies of water were linked with each other and ingress and egress to the smaller one was dependent upon crossing the larger.

The Sammamish River today is a moving current flowing down through the upper end of Lake Washington. It has always been its tributary; the two valleys have been joined since the glacial age. That it was much frequented by tribesmen in fishing seasons has been proven by archaeological discoveries at Marymoor County Park. Here, near the head of the river, Indians from extremely early times gathered to smoke salmon, saturating the earth to a depth of several feet with the grease of their drying fish.

It was natural for landhunters to follow the route of the Indians up the Squowh, or Squak, as the red men called the entire valley of the river and inner lake. Among the four who settled at its head were Mr. and Mrs. William Casto who made their living by cutting poles in the dense hazel thickets. The poles would become barrel hoops and Casto barged loads of them to Seattle to be shipped to San Francisco. He brought back goods to trade to the Indians.

He had been in this business only a year when there was trouble farther up in the foothills; a man named Riley killed three Indians and members of the tribe set out to avenge the deaths. They picked on the Castos as victims and in November, 1864 rushed their cabin and killed the couple while they were at dinner. The other settlers became frightened and made their way out to Lake Washington by trail. It was a year before they returned.

This episode failed to discourage newcomers to the east shore of Lake Washington. It is difficult to place exactly the date of each arrival, but it appears that Aaron Mercer may have been the next after the coal entrepreneurs. The bank of Mercer Slough was the unlikely spot he chose for his homestead.

The Mercer family were well known in pioneer days, but not so much Aaron. It was his two brothers who became locally celebrated. They came from a large family associated with the woolen mills of Mercertown, Ohio. Aaron was born in 1824 and when he was ten his father moved to Princeton, Ill.

Aaron Mercer, the man for whom Mercer Slough was named because he took a land claim beside it. *Seattle Times photo*

In April, 1852 a train of 20 wagons was organized at Princeton to cross the plains to Oregon. Among those in it were Dexter Horton, Daniel Bagley, William H. Shoudy and Aaron and Thomas Mercer. Thomas was elected captain.

Soon after they arrived in Oregon Tom's wife died. Leaving his orphaned daughters with the Hortons, he went to Washington Territory to look for land. He located a donation claim on Lake Union and the next March moved his family to Seattle. He was the first to bring a wagon to King County. At a picnic on July 4, 1854 Thomas suggested that Lakes Washington and Union be given their present names and it is believed that fellow pioneers in turn honored him by christening Mercer Island. Thus the slough and the island were not named for the same man.

At this time Aaron was far away. He had gone to Salem, Ore., where his first wife died and he married Ann Stoven, a young English girl who crossed the plains in the same wagon train. They moved to Grants Pass during the Southern Oregon gold rush. In 1864 they again took the trail and

Aaron drove his wagon north to the Puget Sound country, where Thomas was prospering and had become a leading citizen. This was the year when the youngest brother, Asa, was bringing his famed "cargo of brides" to Seattle.

No one knows why Aaron chose to seek land on the east side of Lake Washington when other members of his family remained closer to Seattle. He settled on 80½ acres on the west bank of Mercer Slough. His other boundaries are today the equivalent of 112th Ave. S.E. on the west and Southeast 24th on the north. His southern line was the shore of the lake, which then extended farther inland. High water covered the present Bellevue Way in that area. Aaron's house was about half a mile up the arm from the main lake and overlooked the expanse that became blueberry farms. It was then flooded, with reeds growing along the edges, fish and beaver and other water denizens inhabiting the slough.

The Mercers occupied a primitive log cabin, their family increasing to 11 children, one of whom drowned in infancy. Upon receiving his homestead patent in 1871, Mercer sold immediately to Susannah Bagley and Dexter Horton. It was a time of much land excitement, coal mining was booming, a railroad through Snoqualmie Pass was a possibility and the Northern Pacific was about to select a terminal city.

Amasa Galloway, owner of property on the other side of Mercer Slough, transferred title to his land the same day as Mercer, although his patent did not come through until nearly a year later. In his case the buyer was James McNaught, attorney for the Northern Pacific, another gambler in land futures.

Part of Mercer's reason for moving was the lack of schools. He bought a place on the Duwamish River, later trading it for property in Oregon. Years afterward he returned to Puget Sound, dying at South Park in 1903. His widow lived until 1919, at which time she was said to have more direct descendants than any other woman in King County. Eight of her children were still living, she also had 44 grandchildren and 30 great grandchildren.

The McGilvras and Others

From Seward Park to Madison Park there was nothing except forest and the Indian camp at Leschi, dubbed Fleaburg by the whites because of its abundance of small livestock.

Madison Park attracted John J. McGilvra, whose house was the only substantial one on the Seattle shore of the lake. He was a New York lawyer who moved to Washington Territory to become its United States attorney. After leaving Olympia for Seattle he served in the legislature. He acquired his lakeshore property when sections of school land were sold to finance the University of Washington. The price was $5 an acre. McGilvra bought 420 acres on both sides of Madison Street, the tract being separated from Seattle by a belt of dense forest. Through this he cleared a winding road from the end of the existing route which reached only to the J.H Nagle farm on Denny Way.

The crude wagon trail was opened in 1864 and in 1867 McGilvra moved his family into Laurel Shade, the residence he built at present 1500 42nd Avenue N. As late as 1880 the McGilvras still were the only

The lake was surrounded by dense woods. Logging was an occupation of the few inhabitants. *University of Washington Library.*

Madison Park when it was John J. McGilvra's farm.

persons living in the Madison Park section. Thomas W. Prosch, the historian, was impressed by the character of McGilvra, whom he described as "a pioneer who chose to go out and take new land, build the first wharf and the first vessel large enough to need government papers." The vessel was a barge.

Shortly after the family moved in the Indians appeared, walking into the kitchen unannounced, squatting on their haunches and demanding coffee or anything else that took their fancy. Among them was one known as Casto Joe because he wore the late Mr. Casto's best coat. It was generally assumed the Indian had taken part in the killing of the couple, though this was unlikely to have been true.

Mrs. McGilvra put up with the annoyance of these unwanted visitors for a long time because she feared to antagonize them. Finally her patience was exhausted and she laid down the law in Chinook jargon in a discourse the like of which they had never heard from a woman. They listened in awe-stricken silence before making a dignified departure in the direction of Seattle.

Halfway to town they met McGilvra, headed for home. They hailed him and said he had better hurry because his squaw was *hyas potlum*, very drunk.

Mrs. McGilvra never experienced trouble with the Indians again; on the contrary, they frequently brought her gifts of fish, clams and berries, which she regularly refused, knowing that acceptance would result in unreasonable demands from the donors.

Far to the south of Laurel Shade, in what is now Uplands Addition back of Seward Park, Walter Graham was another early lakeshore settler. He had participated in the battle of Seattle during the Indian War and his initial employment in the settlement, on his arrival in 1853, was handling logs with a canthook at the Yesler Mill. He was an athlete by pioneer standards, champion collar-and-elbow wrestler on Puget Sound and noted for his prowess in the big jump on the barn floor.

He had taken a land claim in the Duwamish Valley, but Indian troubles sent him away from there and he enlisted in a volunteer military company. Indians destroyed his home.

After marrying Thomas Mercer's daughter, Eliza, Graham became desirous of moving closer to town. His brother, David, a teacher, in 1858 had acquired part of a claim on Lake Washington homesteaded by E.A. Clark, another teacher. In 1863 Walter traded his old claim in the Duwamish for David's smaller one on the lake. Eliza had died the preceding autumn and in 1864 Walter married Katherine Stickney, one of the eleven girls Asa Mercer brought from the East on his first expedition to supply brides to the settlers of Washington Territory.

Next year Graham sold Asa Mercer 100 acres of his farm, but the latter owned it little more than four years when it went to John Wilson in payment for a debt. Wilson at once built his home on the tract, which later was the site of the Martha Washington School. Wilson was a farmer from Massachusetts who with his wife made the voyage to the Pacific Coast on the same ship with Asa Mercer's second expedition. Mercer ran out of funds in San Francisco and Wilson loaned him $1,500 to bring the party on to Seattle. Asa repaid him by deeding the land.

Meanwhile Graham remained on his lake property until 1873, then moved to Seattle to be closer to schools. Although he never owned it, the Seward Park Peninsula was in early days referred to as Graham's Peninsula.

Another pioneer on the lakeshore was Joseph Dunlap, who came to Rainier Beach in September, 1869. He had crossed the plains from Iowa and had been through several Indian skirmishes on the way. A family story relates that on reaching Seattle he drove his covered wagon toward Beacon Hill and told his 14-year-old son, George, to climb a tree and report what was on the other side. George told him about the lake and said the place looked good, so Joseph decided to head for it. He took a homestead of 120 acres, but built his large white frame house well inland, between Henderson and Cloverdale Streets at 47th Avenue South.

Across the lake at what is now Bellevue William Meydenbauer, Seattle baker, was attracted by the possibility of homesteading timber land. A German, who had been apprenticed to a confectioner in his youth, he had come to the West Coast because of the California gold mines. There he lost his stake and returned to Germany and married. Once again he journeyed to America and to Puget Sound and in 1869 because of the beginning of the railroad boom. Seattle then had a population of 900 and business was not sufficiently rushing to keep him tied to his shop. So he rowed to the east side of the lake and staked out 80 acres lying between the head of Meydenbauer Bay and Main Street, Bellevue. He built a cabin and lived in it only enough to prove up on the land. Meanwhile Seattle was growing, the bakery business was thriving, so Meydenbauer did no more with his property, selling it in two sections, the last in 1890. When he tried to buy back a small piece for a vacation cottage he was scandalized at the price he would have to pay for a bit of his old waterfront, $75 an acre!

The first to be attracted to the valley of the Sammamish River were two bachelors, George R. Wilson and Columbus Greenleaf, who canoed up as far as Bothell in 1870 and homesteaded. Several others followed that same year, stayed short periods and sold out. John R. Blyth purchased one of the tracts, at Wayne Golf course in 1872. Next to him,

Houghton in early days. *University of Washington Library*

toward the lake, was Mattias Bargquist, arriving about four years later.

These were all solitary men, but early in 1871 a family moved upstream towed by a rowboat as far as present Woodinville. Ira and Susan Woodin took an 80-acre preemption (the right to purchase government land). She was the first white woman in the valley. Her home became post office, school and Sunday school and her husband later opened a store.

When Mrs. Woodin wanted to go shopping or sell produce for many years her only recourse was to walk a trail through the timber more than three and a half miles to Juanita, from which point she paddled or rowed across the lake. Often she had to return home after dark, carrying a lantern. This was the route over which the mail also went to the settlers on the river, one of them fetching it from Seattle.

Springing up along the shore were the beginnings of Houghton and Juanita, the latter first called Hubbard.

Mrs. Nancy Popham McGregor and her sons, Tom and James Popham, acquired claims at the head of Yarrow Bay in 1871. (Their location was soon to be known as Northup Landing.) The next year Samuel and Harry French settled on 80 acres north of them at Curtis Landing, which became Houghton. The Pophams did not stay long and the Frenches are referred to as the first permanent settlers there. (A house Harry French built in 1874 has lately been moved five blocks to a new site and reconditioned.)

Juanita came into the picture a little later, sometime before 1874. One of the first inhabitants was Charles Dunlap, son of Joseph Dunlap on Rainier Beach.

The Land Speculators

Before leaving this period one must speak of a trio of wealthy land speculators who acquired large sections of the waterfront with an eye to capitalizing on their timber. They were Philip Ritz, Marshall Blinn and Henry Webster, none of whom ever lived in Seattle or anywhere in King County.

Ritz, a Pennsylvanian who had followed the gold rush to California and eventually opened a tree nursery in Walla Walla, made a number of investments around Lake Washington. Between 1867 and 1871 he bought 351 acres on Mercer Island and the 150 acres comprising Seward Park. Both were school land for which he paid $1.25 an acre. Another of his investments was 40 acres of swamp and timber on Portage Bay. His other scattered Lake Washington holdings included some near Sand Point, Wetmore Slough, Denny Blaine and Brighton Beach. He also had land on Lake Union and in downtown Seattle. He hung onto the property through difficult depression periods and some of it was still in the family in the 1950's, although Ritz himself died in 1889 in Walla Walla. The town of Ritzville is named for him. William Bailey bought the Seward Park tract in 1889 from his widow. It was then almost an island.

The big woods in logging days.

Three miles of waterfront on the east shore belonged to Marshall Blinn, founder of a sawmill at Seabeck about 1857. South of Arrowhead Point stretched his timber domain, more than 1,000 acres lying between there and Finn Hill. He acquired some of it in 1872 direct from the government and some from homesteaders. In 1871 he also became the owner of Hunts Point.

That same year he earned unique distinction by establishing two ice houses on Puget Sound and preparing to import ice from Sitka and sell it commercially. To his surprise, he found no ice at the Alaska town, so instead took on board squared timbers and pilings which proved a more profitable investment. He served a term in the territorial legislature and ran for Delegate to Congress but lost the race although he spent a great amount of money for a flamboyant campaign. It seems he was only successful when he stuck to logging, sawmilling and operating lumber-carrying vessels. He died in 1889.

Henry Webster may have been inspired by Blinn when it came to acquiring lake waterfront, of which he eventually owned five and one half miles. Webster lived in Port Townsend and when he moved to Washington he operated a trading post at Neah Bay, becoming the first Indian agent stationed there. He was an astute businessman and must have become infected with the premise that the coming of the railroads would do something for lakeshore property values. Sometime in the 70's he arranged for an employee, John Maggs, to patent a timber claim at Webster Point in Laurelhurst and bought it from him. He also acquired another 8,000 feet of shoreline north of it, and additional acreage between Medina and Evergreen Point and 20 more acres Maggs had proved up on near Seward Park. These came into the hands of his widow, Mary, after his death in 1883.

Another big owner of property on the East Side was the Northern Pacific Railroad, but this derived from government grants along its proposed right-of-way.

Although landseekers were busily laying claim to acreage at a considerable distance beyond the eastern shore, Seattle was still separated from Lake Washington by a band of forest. Dozens of determined men in the 1870s roamed the woods in all directions in quest of timber claims and little log cabins remained in widely scattered places after they had clinched ownership rights and departed. Many quickly sold out or leased logging privileges to others and their names have been lost except in old title records. Relatively few remained to join the list of founding settlers who late in the decade began farming in the clearings and building permanent homes.

Visions of a Canal

John McGilvra had the far-sighted conviction that Lakes Union and Washington ultimately should be linked by a canal, which would continue on to salt water. In 1867 representatives of the Army Corps of Engineers looked over the suggested route and said it was possible, but made no recommendations. Again in 1871 the Army Engineers were back, making a topographical survey of two proposed outlets for such a canal, both leading from the south end of Lake Union. One route would have crossed Thomas Mercer's property.

Col. Thomas H. Handbury, who had charge of the work, was looking for broad uses to justify the expense other than merely remedying periodic floods plaguing farmers in the direction of the Duwamish. In his report he observed that the country around Lake Washington was thickly covered with valuable fir, spruce and cedar.

"On the borders of the lake alone there is enough of the best quality of these species to supply all the wants of the naval depot for years to come," he wrote.

He said Lake Washington was seven feet higher than Lake Union. In dry seasons it was one and one-half feet below normal and in wet seasons four feet above. He found the water, though fresh and soft, not sufficiently pure for drinking because it seemed impregnated with minute particles of decaying vegetable matter and animal life.

The colonel visualized the lake as a fresh-water basin for Navy warships, with torpedo boats "exercising there under steam" and a vast number of naval craft lying at anchor. Of course, he conceded, a means of access first would have to be provided, some channel better than the one then in use by way of the Duwamish and Black Rivers.

Coal had assumed great importance in Seattle's economy and the city fathers were hoping its availability might influence the selection of their port as the terminus for the Northern Pacific Railroad.

The coal had to be moved faster than by the tedious route down the Duwamish, and so the idea of a canal to bring it to Lake Union and on to the city evolved.

In the wagon train crossing the plains in 1852 with the Rev. Daniel Bagley, Aaron and Thomas Mercer was John Henry Pike, a carpenter and contractor from New Hampshire. Pike remained on the Columbia River with relatives until, through Bagley and Asa Mercer, he heard he might secure the contract for building Seattle's Territorial University. He accordingly moved north. Employed with him on the structure was his son, Harvey, who did the painting.

The east end of the canal Pike didn't succeed in building.
Seattle Public Library

That same year of 1861 young Harvey Pike obtained a deed to a tract of public land in present Montlake, including the lower half of the isthmus at the portage and the area around the Seattle Yacht Club and the Museum of History and Industry.

Harvey all his life harbored an urge to build canals. He realized very early the benefits that would ensue from connecting the two lakes and he had the foolhardiness to try accomplishing it almost unaided.

He reserved through his tract a 200-foot-wide strip for a canal crossing from Portage Bay approximately along the route of the present Evergreen Point Bridge approach. This was low marshy land which he imagined he could excavate with pick, shovel and wheelbarrow. He soon realized that it was too big a task for one man's muscle.

Instead of giving up completely, he hung on and awaited developments, knowing that a coal-and-railroad boom was in the making. When the Coal

Creek mine opened in 1869 he platted Union City, a paper town surrounding the south side of the Montlake portage, over which the coal would have to cross to reach Seattle. On the plat he marked the line of his proposed Union Canal, 1,637 feet in length, with several bends in it. The plat was made the same year the Northern Pacific had a reconnaissance party in the field seeking a terminus on Puget Sound. The group went to inspect the newly-opened mine.

In July, 1870, young Pike granted a concession to three men to build a 30-foot-wide road between the lakes until such time as the canal was constructed.

The following month plans were announced for a new rail-and-water method of transporting the coal. Instead of hauling by road from Newcastle to the lake, three and a quarter miles of tramway would bring the mineral down to the east shore, where it would be loaded on barges.

An old resident told of going over that route in 1877. "We got off the little steamboat from Leschi at Hazelwood, or Murphy's Landing, where the narrow gauge line brought the coal down. Two little locomotives were on the run from there to Newcastle. It was a long climb up the first steep mile at Hazelwood. There was quite a settlement on top of the hill. The coal cars were small and the train always backed down to the lake and dumped into the tipple one at a time."

From here the barges were towed to the Montlake portage, where another quarter-mile section of tramway at Pike's Union City was to transport the coal to Lake Union. It would be boated to the south end of Lake Union and would go from there by the last section of tramway to bunkers on the waterfront.

In January, 1871 Pike deeded his property to the Lake Washington Canal Co., which incorporated for the purpose of digging the canal. The promoters petitioned Congress for a donation of land to finance their plan. What they sought was title to the then-submerged lands in Lakes Washington and Sammamish which might be reclaimed when the canal was built. They estimated this at 3,000 acres. The petition made no impression on Congress and Harvey Pike, one of the incorporators, turned to other lines of business. For a time the canal proposed went into limbo.

Rails to the Coal Mines

The new scheme for handling coal was a great improvement over the barges. Up to this time there had been no other craft upon the lake except canoes and rowboats. As early as 1869 the Territorial Legislative Council authorized operation of a ferry, but nothing came of it and the little steamer *James Mortie* was the first engine-driven boat to appear on this body of water. Whether she ever pulled coal barges is in doubt, but she did figure in regular passenger service to the mine landing, leaving the end of Yesler Street on the Seattle side every morning at 9 o'clock. She was a propeller of 4.40 tons registry and was apparently brought up to the lake during the season of high water in the late spring of 1872. Her stay on Lake Washington amounted only to two years, then she was taken back to the Sound.

Meanwhile the coal company acquired the 74-foot sternwheeler *Chehalis* to tow its barges over the new route and she began running sometime in 1872. It was a big day in Seattle when all the links in the portage system for handling the coal were completed and a railroad was ready to take the cars from Lake Union to the waterfront. The first steam locomotive on Puget Sound, the Ant, was brought from San Francisco and installed on the narrow gauge track. The diminutive engine weighed seven tons and had eight small wheels and a tall smokestack. It could pull eight coal cars at a time.

This train only went to the shore of Lake Union. Another steamer brought the cars on a scow from the end of the portage tramway at Montlake. Altogether the coal was handled eleven times between the mine and the ship that would carry it out of Seattle.

The most prominent objects on the Seattle waterfront were the bunkers and trestles of the Seattle Coal and Transportation Co. The structures extended 800 feet into the bay at the foot of Pike Street. Arrival of the first shipment at the bunkers was a gala event, free rides all day long having been offered wheeling through the woods to the waterfront. This was the first railroad excursion on Puget Sound.

During construction of the new coal route the Northern Pacific had chosen Tacoma for its terminus and some time was to pass before the idea of building a canal was revived. Residents of Seattle, however, were determined to have a railroad and they began building a route by hand from Georgetown toward Renton. In May, 1874 they organized the Seattle & Walla Walla Transportation Co.

Renton by then had assumed importance as another coal center. Smithers, the early farmer who located there, was out hunting deer one day and keeping his eyes open for coal indications when he encountered promising float in a creek. Ascending higher up the stream, he used his pick and uncovered a vein. He succeeded in interesting Captain William Renton, of the Port Blakely sawmill, in financing opening the deposit, which afterward was referred to as the Renton mine and gave the town its name.

The site is believed to have been up a steep gully approximately one-eighth mile south of the present

Renton bunkers after the railroad came.
University of Washington Library.

Interpace brick company plant. The original Renton mine community stood on the clay products firm's site. Nearly all of the Smithers claim was deeded by his widow in May, 1874 to the Renton Coal Co., in addition to the clay company site, which had been acquired by Smithers outside of his claim.

Two years after the Renton mine was launched the Talbot mine, a mile south of town, was opened. Coal still went down Black River on barges. Smithers had a horse-drawn tramway, which was improved in 1875 when a narrow-gauge locomotive replaced the animals. How it got there was quite a feat. The engineer, David Jones, ran the engine through Seattle to Lake Union on the coal railroad, loaded it on a barge, portaged it over the isthmus at Montlake, placed it on another flatboat and took it down the lake and into Black River as far as the Black River bridge, constructed in 1867, the first span in King County. (It was just north of the highway intersection at Third and Rainier Avenues.)

Indians made up the audience which watched the locomotive being unloaded and set on the wooden rails of the two-mile-long tramway. This structure facilitated movement of coal to barges operating up and down the Duwamish.

For more than two years the *Chehalis* was alone on Lake Washington, but by January, 1875 she was in trouble. During a windstorm she lost a train of 18 loaded cars, each carrying two tons of fuel. A sudden lurch of the barge careened them off into 200 feet of water opposite McGilvra's Landing and they represented a loss of about $2,000 besides slowing production until more cars could be built.

That was a hard luck season for the *Chehalis*, for in April her engine was nearly destroyed. Early in June the Seattle Coal Co. purchased another vessel, the *Addie*, built for the firm's competitor, the Renton Coal Co.

The year 1875 must have been memorable for officers of the Seattle Coal Co. Business was stopped nearly two weeks in January because of extremely cold weather and a thick layer of ice on Lake Union. The firm could not wait longer for a thaw, so employed a dozen men cutting a channel through the ice for passage of the steamer from the portage.

At first the tramlines on the lake employed horses to draw the cars, but they were gradually replaced with small locomotives. A stage line now ran from the city to the Renton mines, but this ended and so did the barging of coal down the Duwamish when the Seattle & Walla Walla rail line reached Renton in March, 1877. The first cargo of coal was brought to the city by train on March 7. This was such an impressive improvement in the shipping of the fuel that the operators at Newcastle were immediately alerted. Their trestle incline on the Seattle waterfront had caved in, doing considerable damage, and the company needed no persuasion to see the advantages of hooking up to the new railroad. The day after the accident the company let a contract for construction of a branch line from Renton to Newcastle. Three hundred Chinese laborers were brought in to clear the grade and lay track. Timbers were got out for a bridge at May Creek 120 feet high and 70 feet long. While the work progressed Seattle Coal was having a difficult time delivering cargoes to ships and kept trains running over its three short roads all hours of the night.

At the end of January, 1878 the last coal had been moved from Newcastle by barge and portage, the locomotives were sold, the portage rails torn up and preparations were being made to break up the little coal cars and sell them for firewood. All the coal was going into the south end of Seattle by train direct to an enlarged wharf, where the reliable old Ant was serving as switching locomotive. The city's prosperity was greatly increased as a result of this thriving trade from all three coal companies.

The locally built railroad was purchased before 1882 by Henry Villard of the Northern Pacific and renamed the Columbia and Puget Sound Railroad. It was extended to other mines opened at Black Diamond and Franklin. Coal continued to be the Lake Washington region's big industry, but the lake itself was no longer vital to the movement of fuel. The little steamers that had plied its waters and those of the Duwamish were brought back to the Sound and sold to other trades.

The Log Sluice

Logs were another product of the lake country that had to be moved, as the sawmills were mostly outside on Puget Sound. One was operating on Lake Union.

Before there were towboats on the lake tedious hand methods of moving the timbers were resorted to. One logger from the Sammamish River worked his way by carrying an anchor ahead of his raft, using a rowboat. He would drop the anchor, winch his logs up to it, pick up the anchor again, row ahead another cable length and repeat the process.

The woodsmen would form rafts at the foot of skid roads or chutes and when conditions were favorable they would take the logs toward Black

An early sawmill on Lake Union.

Logs going down the Montlake ditch.

River and drive them through the tortuous channels to the Sound.

There was constant pressure among loggers to revive interest in digging a canal. Thus it was that in 1883 David Denny, Thomas Burke, F.H. Whitworth, H.B. Bagley and C.C. Phinney formed the Washington Improvement Co., capitalized at $50,000. Its purpose was to dig the desired waterway, but the contractor to whom the job was let abandoned the undertaking when part way along. There was a temporary interruption in the work before the company hired other men and, with the aid of oxen, scrapers and Chinese labor, within a year completed a small ditch near Harvey Pike's proposed winding route. The passage was just large enough so that logs could be sent through to Lake Union. At the head of the ditch was a board sluiceway with four small floodgates allowing high water to spill over. This was the best the company could accomplish, since Congress ignored pleas to aid the canal project.

How logs were guided through the first canal between Lakes Washington and Union. This photo from a stereo slide owned by the *Seattle Historical Society* was made in 1906.

The log passage, guillotine gate, on Lake Washington end.
Seattle Historical Society

Another view of the log canal.

When rowboats were the main means of transportation on Lake Washington. Photo by Frank LaRoche, a professional photographer who lived in Seattle during the late 1880s and early 1890s. *University of Washington Library*

More Boats Appear

Boats were at a premium in early days on the lake because of the difficulty in reaching it with anything except a flat-bottomed craft or a canoe, due to the shoal at the head of Black River.

The next powered vessel to appear after the *Chehalis* and the *Addie* was the *Minnie Mae*, a 44-footer which ran up the Sammamish River. Freight was carried from the Union City portage and from McGilvra's Landing at the end of Madison Street. Going up, the boat stopped at Sand Point, Whiskey Point (Arrowhead) and Hound House Point (Inglewood) then continued on the winding stream as far as Woodinville.

A few years later J.C. O'Connor's *Squak* became the best known means of transportation on the Sammamish. In winter, when the valley was flooded, the skipper could not find the channel at night or in the persistent fogs, so he simply tied to a snag or a bush until visibility improved.

The *Squak* made her debut in 1884. She was a scow with a house on her, built at Houghton, and her measurements were 42.4 feet length, 14.2 feet beam and 2.6 feet depth. She made the same stops as the *Minnie Mae*, sometimes including the Carkeek brickyard near Mathews Beach, the Lake Forest road and Wayne. Her biweekly trips to Issaquah continued until 1892, when a Christmas day storm broke her up at Kirkland where she was moored.

Travel on most of the lake during the 1880s was haphazard. One either rowed across or boarded a scow sometimes carrying cattle, as farmers on the Seattle side were prone to graze livestock on the north end of Mercer Island and took them back and forth by this means.

Late in the 1880s the *Bee* (built at Eagle Harbor in 1883), the *Edith E.*, the *Jennie June* and the *Evril* were available. The *Edith E.* was built at Houghton in 1886 by W.W. Easter, who operated it. She was a 39 footer of 11.88 tons and named for Easter's wife. Another old-timer was the steam scow *Laura Maud*, launched by O'Connor in 1887. The steamer *Kirkland*, 64.53 tons, was constructed in 1888 also by O'Connor.

These craft on occasion took passengers from the East Side to Leschi or McGilvra's Landing. The *Evril's* captain charged 75 cents for a one-way crossing. His boat was a 30-footer and when Captain James Fairburn had to make a trip down Black River in her he sometimes hired a farmer's ox team to tow her across the bar at the edge of the lake.

Steamer Squak - The first steamboat to operate from Madison Park across to the Sammamish River and what was called Squak Slough. It was of extremely shallow draft. *Photo Seattle Historical Society.*

The ferryboat Kirkland. President Harrison was taken for a cruise on it in 1891.

The Lake Shore & Eastern Railroad

When the ditch for sluicing logs was under construction another momentous project was going on nearby. In 1887 the first section of rails on the Seattle, Lake Shore & Eastern Railroad was laid beyond Lake Union.

This railroad was the creation of Daniel H. Gilman, a New York attorney, who came to Washington in the autumn of 1883 to see if he could develop a coal mine owned by his brother, A.H. Gilman, at what is now Issaquah. Daniel Gilman succeeded in interesting Minneapolis investors in opening the mine, but his first need was a means of transporting the coal to market. Sammamish Slough looked to him impractical as a water route and he concluded that a railroad would have to be built.

He found ample support for this idea among such Seattle business leaders as Judge Thomas Burke, A.A. Denny and Henry Yesler, who wanted to move his logging operations to Lake Washington. But Denny and Burke had other fish to fry. Both were interested in iron mines several miles west of the summit of Snoqualmie Pass and eager to promote them.

Denny claimed to have discovered the iron after seeing Indians use a black face paint. He persuaded an old Indian to show him the source of the stuff and found it was a deposit of magnetic iron ore and red hematite. As a consequence, in 1872 and 1873 several prospectors filed on mineral claims, among them A.A. Denny, Wilson Denny, F.M. Guy, Charles K. Jenner and James Taylor. In 1884 Denny and some of the others incorporated.

Gilman lost no time in getting the railroad project on its feet. Nothing deterred him. A New York bank collapsed and several of his stockholders were ruined. Gilman tried again, examined his scheme and promised that the railroad would cross the mountains without need of a tunnel and would reach Spokane Falls. Gilman had to make three trips to New York before he succeeded in bringing Eastern capitalists out to look over the ground and convinced them late in 1886 that he should go ahead.

It was on this third trip that Gilman met Peter Kirk, representing the Moss Bay Hematite Iron and Steel Co. of Workington, Cumberland, England, the firm which was to supply the rails. Gilman told Kirk about the abundance of coal and iron near Seattle and offered to show him the deposits, to determine if he wanted to acquire the mines for his company.

Kirk and John Kellett, engineer with his firm, journeyed west and visited Denny's iron mine and Guy's, in which Judge Burke was a partner. Kirk quickly was sold on the proposition of erecting a Bessemer steel plant similar to the one with which he was involved in England. He went home and disposed of his holdings.

In the meantime Gilman busied himself with obtaining donations of the railroad right-of-way, surveying crews went out in the field, and 5,000 tons of rails were ordered from Workington.

The railroad station site on the Seattle waterfront was secured from Henry Yesler and the line of tracks was planned to run north to Smith Cove, and behind Queen Anne Hill to Salmon Bay, thence across a small stream to Fremont and along the north shore of Lake Union almost to the portage. It would cut along the lower end of the present University of Washington campus, swing toward the shore and make a horseshoe bend at Union Bay.

Getting any railroad started was a big feat in the face of opposition from the Northern Pacific, which had selected Tacoma for its terminus. Gilman was accused of having a "paper" railway and for a time it looked as though the line was indeed all promotion and no rails. The iron was being shipped on three or more vessels from England and the first of them, the *Rhydalmere*, was 77 days getting around Cape Horn.

The delay greatly embarrassed the local promoters and they were ready to stage a big celebration when the second ship, the *Persian*, docked on August 12, 1887 and brought news that the rest of the rails would soon arrive. There was a ceremony at Smith Cove of removing some of the rails from the *Persian*, laying them on the wharf, driving the first spike and drenching the initial rail in champagne.

With all speed crews got to work and a portion of the line was ready when two locomotives arrived in June, their tenders bearing the names "D.L. Gilman" and "H.L. Yesler." Excitement was high, as it appeared certain that as soon as the rails reached the coal mines and the iron mines beyond them, Kirk would have a foundry in operation. Tacoma tried to lure him there, but he was bound by contracts to the original plan.

He had entered a lease agreement with Denny stipulating that at least 30,000 tons of ore annually be mined and the products were to go through Seattle for shipment or sale. His contract with the Guy mine owners was to be an outright purchase for $30,000, under the obligation to ship all ore on the Seattle, Lake Shore & Eastern.

Gilman continued to make far-reaching plans. He paid visits to Colfax and Walla Walla and spoke of rails tapping those regions. Tacoma, alert to his activities, went on jeering about Gilman's railroad "built of wind."

On September 9, 1887 newspapers told of the

Seattle, Lake Shore and Eastern tracks north of the present university campus. *Seattle Historical Society.*

first inspection trip over the new road, from the wharf to the end of track on Lake Washington. The train passed over a long trestle at Smith Cove, then through a stretch of timber for a short distance before reaching Salmon Bay, which the track skirted for half a mile. It crossed to the north side of Lake Union on a short trestle, then pierced the timber once more, emerging on the Lake Washington shore and running four miles along it.

"Though the road is yet unballasted," the account stated, "the train bearing the inspecting party was run at the rate of 30 miles an hour, and that, too, without inconvenience. It may be safely said that the completed portion of the Seattle, Lake Shore & Eastern Railroad is the most substantially built piece of railroad on the Pacific Coast." The reporter observed that when completed "it will compare favorably for smoothness and for its substantial nature with the oldest and best equipped roads of the East."

Gilman announced that the next 40-mile division would be commenced within a few weeks and that in 12 months 50 miles more, possibly 300 miles, would be built.

Work of opening the coal mines at Squak (Issaquah) was progressing under the superintendence of F.H. Whitworth and a large amount of coal would be ready for shipment as soon as the rails reached there. Mines owned by the Seattle Coal & Iron Co. would also be opened that year at Raging River.

Meanwhile property had been purchased at Smith Cove comprising 700 acres, which were to be

Houses in Yesler on Union Bay, 1893. *Seattle Public Library.*

platted. Coal bunkers would be built as soon as the road reached the Squak mines.

The line arrived at Bothell* on Thanksgiving Day, 1887 and at Woodinville soon afterward. Then it took off south through the Sammamish Valley and around the east shore of Lake Sammamish and was in Issaquah the next year. It went on through Preston, Fall City, Snoqualmie and North Bend. The immediate destination was Sallal Prairie, 2.5 miles east of North Bend, where Kirk had seriously considered erecting his foundry.

In 1888 the Denny and Guy iron mines each had opened a tunnel and they were ready to go into production.

**Note:* George Brackett's logging show was at Bothell and in 1882 he established a camp in the center of the present town, then known as Brackett's Landing. Two years later David C. Bothell, who had logged with ox teams near Lake Union, bought 80 acres from Brackett. After purchasing 40 more acres, Bothell opened a boarding house and later platted the town.

The Upper West Shore

The 1880s had brought many changes and more population to the lakeshore. Roads were improved and extended and stages carried sportsmen to Leschi and McGilvra's Landing at the end of Madison Street, from whence they boated across to indulge in hunting expeditions. Scattered farmers on the east side were gradually bringing crops into bearing and had need to make the long trip to market with their produce. The pioneering period was ended and from there on developments in the communities along the shoreline should be examined separately, beginning with the upper part of the west shore and its new rail line.

After the railroad passed the site of the present Edmundson Pavilion at the University it followed a horseshoe bend around an arm of Union Bay, where the stream from Green Lake, Ravenna Creek, came down through what is now Ravenna Park and poured into a swamp. Here, at the spot where Indians had found good fishing, Henry Yesler, Seattle's first sawmill owner, chose to locate his new mill and the little town of Yesler sprang up near today's Union Bay Place. The University Village shopping center covers the former swamp and the stream flows through an underground conduit and past the University parking lot directly into Union Bay.

Yesler's second sawmill was built in 1888 and stood until September 16, 1895, when it went up in flames. Today the Carnation Co. has a large building just west of the millsite. It is difficult to imagine a log-storage pond where are now paved parking lots. The Seattle Ice Co. factory was across the track near the mill and a tannery stood between the tiny town and Ravenna Park.

A second railroad stop on the bay was Ravenna, at 25th Avenue N.E. and Blakely Street. Nearby Mrs. W.W. Beck, in 1890, opened the Seattle Female Academy. Her husband operated Ravenna Springs Park, charging a 50-cent entrance fee to view the extremely large trees, many of them bearing names of presidents. Some were 50 to 60 feet in circumference and up to 400 feet in height. They mysteriously vanished just prior to the 1920s, either from natural causes or corrupt management of what had become a city park.

No University station existed in early years, as the school did not move from the center of the city to its modern campus until 1895. The grounds then constituted a section of publicly-owned school land covered with virgin forest, though Charles M. Anderson, engineer for the log sluice, claimed a homestead in the vicinity and built a log cabin where the varsity crew house later stood.

Farming, mining and logging benefitted from the new railroad. But sometime in its first year of operation Gilman had to abandon his intention of providing coal from his Squak mine for any foundry that Peter Kirk might build. The Squak coal was excellent for heating houses, but no good for coking.

Gilman, Burke and their associates, instead of carrying the rails over Snoqualmie Pass, organized a branch line toward the Canadian border, by way of Snohomish. Their intention was to form a junction with the Canadian Pacific Railroad and thus achieve their first transcontinental connection. They had hopes that if they waited, the Great Northern would be extended from Montana to Spokane and they could reach an understanding with that company about taking over and crossing through Snoqualmie Pass.

An engineer exploring for the Great Northern had been a distinguished guest on that first inspec-

School at Yesler.

Excursion train in the gay 90's. Note the timber close to the tracks. *Seattle Historical Society photo.*

Colonsay, the house built on Webster Point in Laurelhurst by Wilbur A. McNeill. This first residence in the area is still standing, though closely surrounded by other homes. *Seattle Times photo.*

tion ride over the Seattle, Lake Shore & Eastern route.

There couldn't have been much passenger service over the new railroad at first, but cargoes of logs made up for the lack of patrons in the stove-heated passenger coaches.

Gradually what had been forests along the west shore of Lake Washington became orchards and farms, especially through Laurelhurst and Windermere. W.H. (Joe) Surber, for whom Surber Drive in Laurelhurst is named, was one of the first comers, beginning in 1890.

Six years later Wilbur A. McNeill, a Scotsman interested in coal properties, acquired 36 acres on Webster Point that had been patented as a timber claim. Mrs. Henry A. Webster, the widow from whom the purchase was made, had inherited two other Laurelhurst plots.

Webster Point was isolated from roads and reached only by boat from the end of Madison Street.

McNeill named his new home Colonsay, for the Scottish island where his mother was born. He was a bachelor in poor health and persuaded his niece to travel out from Scotland and keep house for him, promising to make her his heir. He died late in 1896 after living in his house only a few months. The niece, finding no buyer, closed the place and it was 1906 before it was acquired by a realty firm planning to put Laurelhurst on the market. The McNeill residence and its gardens were photographed from various angles, to give the impression of several different homes, and these pictures were used to illustrate the company's brochure. The house was still the only building in that part of Laurelhurst.

The property sold slowly and not until 1910 were there enough residents to justify annexation to Seattle. The McNeill house still stands on the point, but the grounds have been divided into lots occupied by numerous other homes.

The only other development in Laurelhurst's early years was the Seattle Golf and Country Club, from 1900 to 1907. It installed a landing at 51st Street N.E. and maintained its own boat service for members.

Prior to the present century the goal of summer passengers by boat and train out the west shore, and later by car over the winding road from Ravenna, frequently was Mud Lake at Sand Point, a depression which gave the picnic beach there contours radically different from its present ones.

The lake is gone now. Filled and leveled, it was part of the naval air reservation. Between it and Windermere the large home of Rolland Denny was to rise in 1908, stately and alone on a high bluff above the water. It has lately become headquarters of the Rev. Moon's controversial Unification Church.

On rounding Sand Point, the boatman late in the 1890's would have noted a small village clustered around the Pontiac Brick & Tile Co., where long piles of brick awaited shipment. The next landmark north of Pontiac Bay was the mill of the Maple Leaf Shingle Co., which existed between 1893 and 1900 and gave its name to the district around N.E. 95th Street.

Spur lines for logging ran up from the lakeshore, accounting for such flag stops on the railroad as Hostler, Belden and Lake. Years later, during the First World War, another small shingle mill stood near Pontiac.

The railroad tracks followed the shoreline closely to avoid any grades that would have been necessary had the route taken to the hills. Today houses are below the former roadbed (now the Burke-Gilman Trail) on land reclaimed when the water level was lowered in 1916.

Lake City still was covered with tall timber at the turn of the century and it was about 1916 before the last of it around 145th Street was cut.

In 1904 Clyde C. Chittenden purchased from the Pacific Coast Coal Co. 740 acres lying between N.E. 115th and N.E. 145th Streets. He built a logging camp consisting of cook house, dormitory and store at the section line at N.E. 125th Street. His railroad reached from present Lake City to the lake. Later it extended toward Jackson Park and Olympic Hills. In all of this area there were no roads but those which the logging company constructed and no houses except its own buildings.

Chittenden logs were towed down Lake Washington, sent through the sluice and taken to the Edgewater Mill on Lake Union, just west of the Fremont Bridge. The mill, in which Chittenden had a controlling interest, burned in 1912.

After the area was logged Chittenden turned over the bulk of his property to Homer Hillman, who platted Lake City, Chittenden's Terrace Park, Acacia Cemetery and the shorelands. All of the Chittenden property to N.E. 145th Street is today inside Seattle's limits.

Another logging operation on the same side of Lake Washington was at Lake Forest Park in 1907, when W.J. Rowe erected a sawmill in the valley near the present Lake Forest Park School. Before his day a flume passed through Lake Forest Park, down which floated shingle bolts cut at Lake Ballinger. Much cedar stood throughout here and the Rowe mill cut shingles as well as lumber from these trees.

The North End

Sportsmen used to speak with relish of the days between 1895 and 1905 when wild ducks abounded among the reeds at the mouth of Sammamish River. Then Kenmore was noted for its boathouse and floating landing, its sportsmen's hotel and saloon. In that time there were duck clubs at the edge of the marshes up the river, usually small cabins owned by little groups of affluent citizens, who went by horse and buggy from Kirkland after crossing the lake by steamboat. Using decoys and by putting out feed, they attracted great flocks of teal, mallards and widgeon.

Loggers always were seen at Kenmore and even in recent years logs were unloaded there from trains and stored in rafts. Sill Brothers early in the century had a tramway which ended at the lake near the present seaplane terminal. The tramway rails were poles laid end on end. The logs boomed at this place were floated out to Puget Sound the long way around through Black River and the Duwamish.

At flood seasons the accumulated timbers of loggers at Bothell, Woodinville and Lake Sammamish poured out of the mouth of the Sammamish and these, too, were boomed in the lake and towed away. James Houghton had a log chute near the river in 1886, Verd Brothers logged nearby and N.I. Peterson had another chute in which he sent the big trees he cut on Moorlands Hill down to the water. Peterson logged on the Inglewood Golf Course in 1905 and three other outfits were cutting timber immediately south of him.

From 1900 a sawmill stood north of the modern air harbor. It was erected by the Fir Lumber Co., which sold several years later to John McMasters.

He had a busy establishment with a payroll of 25. McMasters came from a small Canadian town, Kenmore, 40 miles south of Ottawa. He worked in several shingle mills before leasing land from Watson C. Squire, the last territorial governor of Washington.

Squire acquired the land around Kenmore from his father-in-law, Philo Remington, son of the firearms inventor. Remington decided to unload his

Typical lakeshore view before the water was lowered. Photo by A.C. Warner. *University of Washington Library.*

patch of dense forest after the Northern Pacific had chosen Tacoma for its terminal.

McMasters named the logging community for his old home. He operated the mill until 1923, when it was destroyed by fire. Squire died in 1926 and his family carried on improvement of his property, planning to make it into a residential waterfront park. After the end of logging Puget Mill Co., which owned land both east and west of the Squire tract, offered small garden acreage for sale at the end of the First World War. Completion of a highway up the lake in 1913 stimulated growth and restaurants sprang up, causing Kenmore to become a popular dining place.

A wooden bridge was built near the mouth of the Sammamish in 1917 and four years later the Inglewood golf course was opened. The first bridge across the river was farther up, at the Wayne Golf Course, and highway planners considered that the logical route of a future Lake Washington Boulevard.

Nearly everyone living on the lakeshore has a boat of some sort. This scene is at Arrowhead Point. *Photo by Greg Gilbert.*

The Northeast Shore

Farther south on the east shore was Arrowhead, North Point or Whiskey Point. It earned its various names from the fact that Indians hid whiskey there and that arrowheads were dug up in the garden of a early resident, Albert Grant Shears. The little triangle of level land at the foot of a steep slope was initially the homestead of Reuben J. Crocker, who received his patent in 1890. He sold a portion of his property to the Shears in 1893. For many years two small houses occupied the point and were the only signs of habitation between Inglewood and Holmes Point Drive.

Albert Shears owned most of the land until 1939. He was cut off from communication with the outside world except by boat, as no road led down to his place. When he wanted to go to the city he put a white flag on his landing or, if the weather was foggy, he beat on a triangle or old saw blade to signal the Sammamish River boat to come in and pick him up.

Today the entire point from the top of the hill down is fully improved and houses line its many short streets, which feed into Juanita Drive.

South of Arrowhead Point stretched the timber domain of Marshall Blinn. He had acquired 260 acres in 1879 and after his death his widow, Julia, bought another quarter section. These were only part of the Blinn holdings in this neighborhood, but aside from being leased for logging, they remained untouched and were inherited by a grandson of the pioneer timber tycoon. It was not until 1921 that the tract went to owners outside of the family. Five years later the Catholic bishop of Seattle bought it as the site for St. Edward's Seminary, a school where candidates for the priesthood could be trained. As the establishment grew a second seminary, St. Thomas, was erected on the extensive grounds, which by this time were considerably reforested with second growth trees. The two schools, in charge of the Society of St. Sulpice, flourished until attendance began falling off in 1976 and St. Edward's was closed. In another 12 months it was announced that St. Thomas's was destined to shut its doors also and the big expanse of wooded land would become a realty development. This prospect alarmed residents and a campaign was inaugurated to make it a state park. The effort succeeded and now people may picnic where student priests once walked.

Little is known about Blinn's other property to the south of the seminary grounds. Some had been government land he had bought in 1872. When the grandson was 12 years old the probate court arranged for sale of logging rights to the Western Mill Co. Traces of its skid roads were visible near the seminary and Denny Park for many years.

A realty firm, the Lake Park Land Co., bought part of the logged-off acres and, to attract investors in summer home sites, constructed landings north and south of Denny Park and subsidized boat service in the steamship *Acme*, which made stops on the way between Madison Park and Bothell.

The largest purchaser in the Lake Park development was Orion Orville Denny, second son of pioneer Arthur A. Denny. Orion had the distinction of being the first white boy born in Seattle. He became a marine engineer and after 20 years of steamboating joined the Denny Clay Co., which his father had founded. The son succeeded to the presidency of the firm after his parent's death. He never lost his love of the water and owned a palatial yacht, the *Helori*.

Denny purchased 43 acres at Lake Park, with a total of 2,500 feet of waterfront. He erected a port-

Buildings at St. Edwards State Park formerly a Catholic seminary for young men intending to go into the priesthood. *Photo by Greg Gilbert.*

Woods in O.O. Denny Park. *Photo by Greg Gilbert*

The venerable patriarch of Denny Park *Photo by Parker McAllister*

Big firs in O.O. Denny Park. *Photo by Greg Gilbert*

able house and two landings at which he moored his yacht and a launch. The house remained until demolished in 1955.

It was the fashion to give summer homes Indian names, so Denny called his country estate Kla-hanie (Outdoors). After he died in 1916 the property went to his third wife, Mrs. Helen V. Denny. The couple had no children. The widow came to an unhappy end; she married a second time, was divorced and in a despondent mood shot herself in 1922. Before taking her life she willed Kla-hanie to the city of Seattle for a park, with the proviso that it be improved and beautified.

Denny's property is now a public picnic ground. Formerly a separate section was set aside for Camp Denny, where children would be brought from Seattle playgrounds for over-night camping. This enterprise was created in 1926. A playground and camping facilities at Carkeek Park on Pontiac Bay had been given to Seattle by Mr. and Mrs. Morgan J. Carkeek, but in 1922 the federal government bought all of the Sand Point district for a naval air base. Carkeek made a second gift to the city of funds for the present Carkeek Park in northwest Seattle, but the park department decided to salvage the buildings on Pontiac Bay and barge them across the lake to the new Denny property on the East Side. The move proved successful and a typical season at Camp Denny was in 1931 when 2,000 youngsters from Seattle, 55 groups in all, spent a night there.

A few hundred yards up the canyon of Denny Creek stand two ancient Douglas fir trees, which were bypassed by the loggers who left stumps throughout this region as reminders of their early activity. The largest tree is about seven feet in diameter, 26½ feet in circumference and 254 feet high. The bark is 12 inches thick and it is a minimum of 550 years in age. Probably it is the biggest Douglas fir remaining in the immediate vicinity of Seattle. A group of Campfire Girls has placed a commemorative tablet at its base.

Finn Hill, the highest land near Juanita, was the place where the young men in settlers' families nearby generally found employment working for logging companies. Scheaffer Brothers cut most of the trees on the hill. The logs were dragged to a steep chute leading down to Champaign Point, where they were made into rafts.

A story is told that some men in a skiff capsized at the point. It is said they were drunk and for that reason someone named the place for champagne, although the spelling is wrong. Old residents said, no matter, whiskey and not champagne was the root of the trouble.

Until the present century bull-team logging was still in use on the East Side and the last of these oxen was recorded in 1907. Horses and steam donkey engines by then were taking their places in the woods.

Finn Hill's name originated about that period, as it received its first Finnish families in 1906 or 1907. After the first two went there, three more followed until finally some 55 Finnish families were scattered over the hilltop. At least 29 of the homes had saunas, steam baths, in the back yard. The tight little community had its own club house. At the start it was a hardship colony, prepared to exist with very few assets, but these were thrifty folk who kept cows when they had no barns, raised hay and strawberries and other produce, which they walked to Kirkland to sell because they had no horses and vehicles.

When they arrived on the hill it still was covered with the debris of logging and the only roads were those made for that purpose. For a number of years the only persons living there were Finns, except for the family of a retired Seattle postman.

Logging with ox teams east of Renton in 1893. *Darius Kinsey Photo*

Juanita

Long ago, when the level of the lake was higher, Indians used to paddle their canoes to the head of Juanita Bay and gather wapatoes, edible bulbs which were harvested in four or five feet of water. The plants had arrow-shaped leaves and were found in the area where cattails and water lillies now thrive a few feet away from 98th Avenue N.E.

A pioneer resident said, "We used to gather wapatoes as kids and roast them for fun. They tasted a little like sweet potatoes. I saw an occasional canoeload of Indians gather them right up until the time the lake was lowered."

Juanita first was called Hubbard, for a family living in the 1870's on the hill east of the present community. Hubbard, a logger, carried mail from Seattle in his rowboat. When he drowned a few years later off Rose Point, the settlers felt some other name for the locality would be more appropriate, as the landing in the bay was no longer his. It is understood that the selection of Juanita was made by Mrs. Charles C. Terry, of Seattle, whose husband owned land on the south shore. The first white child born in the community in 1879 was christened Juanita Dunlap for her birthplace. She was the daughter of Charles Dunlap, the first school teacher.

The first store in Juanita was opened by Harry Langdon in 1902. Roland Langdon was among the initial settlers, taking a homestead in 1877. Until a few years ago N.E. 116th Street was called Langdon Road.

Another of the pioneers was Dorr Forbes, a Civil War veteran, who in 1877 had taken a preemption

Store at Juanita started by Harry W. Langdon in 1902. *Photo courtesy Minnie Langdon Sabo*

claim on Rose Hill. A bog on the property abounded in wild cranberries and it was no trick to pick a gunny sack full of them. When Forbes tried to improve his land beavers ruined his ditches. Battling the animals was a losing game, so he sold out and moved to Juanita, where by the middle of the 1880s he was operating a small water-powered shingle mill on Juanita Creek.

Forbes dammed the stream to make a log pond and a little fall. The road west of the shopping center crosses the creek where the dam was. From this point it used to be possible to trace the outline of the old mill pond. The mill stood about three blocks north of the beach on property now occupied by a modern home. The mill burned in 1894 after a dry kiln was installed.

Leslie Forbes, son of the sawmill man, recalled, "The ice house still was standing after the fire and we had ice all that summer. We cut the ice in the pond. Winters were cold then and the ice was six to eight inches thick."

Dorr Forbes had a boat landing, where a scow would moor, awaiting a load of shingles to be towed away. Some of the shingle bolts came from cedars left standing on Finn Hill. Farmers would cut them and skid them down to Juanita.

Mrs. Forbes became justice of the peace in 1887. Her son said he never would forget her biggest scare. Half a dozen Indian women tried to enter her home one day when she was alone. "It turned out," Leslie related, "that all they wanted was to warm their bare feet at her stove."

Activities at Juanita changed greatly after lowering of the lake, for this exposed a shallow sandy beach which attracted picnickers and swimmers. Leslie and Edward Nelson decided to profit from this, so in the summer of 1920 they opened a stand selling candies and other refreshments. Leslie also bought from his widowed mother the 30-foot strip of land that had given access to the Forbes dock and an additional two lots. A real estate company owned the waterfront, but the partners were able to lease enough more so that they had the makings of a beach resort. They cleared away the logs, planted cottonwoods for shade, erected "Chic Sales" and built a bath house and dressing rooms. Next came an open-air kitchen and a covered picnic space and the family were in business, renting tables for 25 cents a day. They went on adding to their resort a canoe house, water slide and floodlights on a block-long pier.

These improvements set a pattern and soon Thomas W. Blakeney started another resort, Shady Beach, and Edward Tolmie opened Sandy Beach. In the 1930s 10,000 persons often thronged to Juanita on a hot Sunday. Hamburger stands and dance pavilions did a thriving business.

Twenty-five years in this hectic enterprise were sufficient for the Forbes family and both they and Blakeney turned the beaches over to Joe and Virginia Steiner. In 1956 King County bought the Forbes beach and the following year purchased the family home for part of a new park. Shady Beach was sold to the county in 1958. They are all in one tract today and still a great gathering place for swimmers and picnickers.

Rose Point, south of Juanita Bay, is an attractive Kirkland residential district. It has been variously called Nelson Point and Williams Point in the past for families who have lived there. On early charts of the lake it also appeared as Glandwyr, a Welsh name meaning "By the Water." Here Walter W. Williams of Workington, England, built a cottage for his family's first home in the new country. He had migrated from Great Britain with Peter Kirk in 1888 to become secretary of the latter's steel mill, a position similar to the one he had held at the Workington plant.

Williams later erected a brick home on Waverly Way in Kirkland, but he kept the cottage for use in summers. He died in 1915 and the property came into the hands of a real estate developer. He leased it to two Frenchmen who planned to utilize its pond to raise frogs' legs commercially and sell them to Seattle restaurants. They imported a large species from France, but the frogs escaped through the fences and propagated in the lake, where fishermen gleefully caught them. The owner next tried truck gardening, but eventually the swampy ground was filled and became a golf course. It was used for this purpose until the 1970s.

Originally the street along the shore at the head of the bay was on a trestle. Leslie Forbes remembered when his father cut piling for the structure in the early 1890s and donated the timbers as his contribution toward completing the only road that connected Juanita and Kirkland. These are not the pilings now seen in the water; they remain from a dock built by the City of Seattle for handling gravel in the 1920s.

Boom Days in Kirkland

After 98th Avenue N.E. passes the head of the bay, the thoroughfare takes the name of Market Street. At the intersection of Seventh Avenue are three brick buildings, almost the only remaining relics of Kirkland's great dream. Another, a hotel, stood on the fourth corner, but it was demolished and the bricks were used to construct a service station now occupying the ground.

These structures and the city itself relate to the Peter Kirk story. When Gilman found that he could not sell his coal to the proposed iron foundry and turned his attention to independent developments at Salmon Bay and the northern extension of his railroad, Kirk's project was picked up by new sponsors.

By June 1, 1888 he had definitely given up thought of locating at Sallal Prairie. He had already abandoned his first intention of going to Tacoma where he would have coking coal from the Wilkeson-Fairfax-Carbonado district of Pierce County.

Peter Kirk, for whom Kirkland was named. *Seattle Times photo from collection of Myrtle C. Robertson.*

Kirkland when lake was high · This was taken about 1907 from the hill east of Market Street, evidently between Second and Third Streets. The view was south of today's business center. Buildings now stand where the pond was and the shoreline is more than a block west of Lake Street, which is flanked on both sides by buildings. *Seattle Times photo.*

Leigh S.J. Hunt, publisher of the Post Intelligencer and officer of many Seattle corporations, had focused Kirk's attention upon the east side of Lake Washington as a site for his plant. The coking coal could come just as well from the south, by way of a line the Northern Pacific would build from Black River Junction. Hunt knew where land was available and the first thing to do was form a company to exploit it. That July the firm incorporated and on August 18 the Moss Bay Iron and Steel Co. was formed, with Hunt, Kirk, Williams, Denny, Jacob Furth and H.A. Noble on its board of directors.

In 1889 Kirk went to England to purchase equipment. By the end of the year the new company was short of funds and was reincorporated the following June as the Great Western Iron & Steel Co. That was the year of Seattle's disastrous fire. It was also the year when the idea of a ship canal was revived, with talk of building it from the south end of the lake. Another happening was the incorporation in July, 1880 of the Seattle Iron & Steel Manufacturing Co., to build on the Salmon Bay site. Curiously, Hunt and his father-in-law, Henry A. Noble, were among its incorporators.

The sky seemed to be the limit when it came to promoting iron and steel mills. Those were boom days, although by February, 1890 the Seattle, Lake Shore & Eastern Railroad was rumored near collapse for lack of funds. Receivership proceedings had been instituted against it at Spokane Falls, where stockholders complained the line was not being built east, but north, and that they were being discriminated against. When these efforts to put the company in the hands of a receiver failed, control was secured by purchase of stock from eastern stockholders, the locals having refused to sell any. The Northern Pacific secured two-thirds of the shares.

By March 1890 Gilman had directed his attention to seeking a right-of-way for a subsidiary of the Great Northern and the following month he was out as head of the Seattle, Lake Shore & Eastern. His successor in office was an employee of Gilman's hated enemy, the Northern Pacific.

Another of Gilman's activities that spring was organizing the Salmon Bay Railway and Development Co., to build docks and ship the coal that was to be brought by rail. That was just before he was eliminated from the Seattle, Lake Shore & Eastern. His motives must have been extremely complicated and his financing ephemeral.

Equally as tenuous were the assets of the Great

Western Iron & Steel Co., which had selected for its site the place to be known as Kirkland. The reorganized firm was composed of Kirk, Williams, Hunt, Denny, Noble, Jacob Furth and three out-of state men, Columbus T. Tyler, R.A. Alger and Edward Blewett. Stock certificates pictured Kirkland with an imaginary skyline of smoke-belching factory chimneys and the company announced its purpose "to own, lease and acquire iron, coal and other types of mines, limestone quarries, stone quarries and brickyards, collieries, foundries, rolling mills and works for making coke and reducing ores; to engage in and carry on the trade or business of ironmaster, colliery proprietors, coke manufacturers, mineral smelters, engineers, steel converters and iron founders; to own and operate powers, buildings and machinery for manufacturing motor power, and to construct, maintain and improve water works, gas works, electric light plants, ponds and reservoirs."

Most important to this grandiloquent program was the firm's relationship with the Kirkland Land Co., whose offices it was soon to share in a brick building erected at the foot of Market Street. The land company owned between 1,200 and 1,400 acres on the East Side. Some accounts have placed the figure as high as 5,000 acres. Stockholders included Hunt, Kirk, Williams and Denny.

Peter Kirk always has been credited with being the father of Kirkland. Actually the place was founded by Leigh Hunt. He believed that if it could be made an iron and steel capital, other industries could be lured there. The big thing was to exploit the land. It had cost $100 an acre and the company's expectation was that when platted the same area would bring $1,000.

The company cleared the west side of Kirkland, burned stumps and laid out lots after first donating 120 acres to the steel mill. Kirk called the stretch of water in front of the future town Moss Bay, in memory of the Workington plant on an English Moss Bay. His family had been associated with it since 1869 and he was probably reluctant to see the company lose its first name in the reorganization.

To streets Kirk gave such designations as Bessemer, Piccadilly, Regent, Depot and Bond. His plat showed an elaborate double diamond plaza located two blocks up the Market Street hill. Market was planked nearly to Juanita and Piccadilly (Seventh) was planked to the site of the steel mill, curiously placed on Rose Hill instead of near the water. Enemies of the company accused the stockholders of reserving the waterfront for themselves so they could make more money from sales of the property.

One of the four brick buildings erected at the intersection of Market and Piccadilly was to contain a bank on its lower floor. Planners visualized that this corner would be the hub of the city.

View of the present Arts and Crafts Building, Kirkland, once intended for a bank in Peter Kirk's day. *Photo by Greg Gilbert*

Depot Street had significance, for in 1890 the Northern Pacific began construction of the Lake Washington Belt Line Railroad from Black River Junction. The grade followed the lakeshore on the east side in a general direction, crossing Mercer Slough, going through the eastern portion of Kirkland and on to Woodinville, where it would connect with the Seattle, Lake Shore & Eastern, which was now under Northern Pacific control. In this way it could deliver iron ore from the mines in Snoqualmie Pass and at the same time bring coking coal from the Wilkeson-Fairfax district. The plan called for 22 miles of new railroad, but only five miles of steel were actually laid and these were from the Woodinville end of the route.

It is of passing interest to know that Peter Kirk during his initial activities purchased coal mines a mile north of Green River, not far from Black Diamond and Franklin. He sold them in 1888 after discovering they would not produce coking coal. The question of his supply remained in doubt for some time, but inevitably he had to turn to Wilkeson, where the first coke had been produced in 1880. Influenced by the Tacoma smelter and the proposed one at Kirkland, production was increased until by 1891 Wilkeson had more than 90 coke ovens.

Considerable time had passed since Kirk entered his first agreements with the iron-mine owners and in 1890 he petitioned the Denny Iron Mining Co. to release him from any legal action for breach of contract, due to his failure to begin construction of the smelter within six months of signing the lease.

Its construction at last was under way in June, 1890. Since securing out-of-state assistance the firm was supposed to have a paid-in capital of $1,000,000. In reality only three-fourths of that amount was paid in.

Of this, $200,000 is said to have been invested in mill preparations and construction. Two miles west of the mill, on the lakefront, buildings were erected to receive English shipments of fire clay, fire brick, cement and other materials soon due to arrive.

The year 1891 was a busy one, with all the burning over of cleared land and the construction of brick buildings. A brickyard was opened on the waterfront in the space that is now public parking for Kirkland shoppers. By March a sawmill, installed on the mill property, had cut sufficient lumber for the steel plant. A machine shop, blacksmith shop, pattern department, bunkers and a structure to house a small blast furnace were erected.

Everything appeared ready for commencing operations when work closed down in September, 1892, ostensibly for the winter. The doors never reopened for business.

Suddenly Kirkland was at a standstill—the enterprise that was to have employed 2,000 men was locked up, the plank streets were empty and rail construction stopped. Rumors were circulated about various dire happenings. But there must have been an undercurrent of expectation, for 1892 was the year when the Seattle Chamber of Commerce counted upon the Lake Washington Ship Canal and locks to be built. The Kirkland mill would be dependant upon the canal for ships bringing in limestone from the San Juan Islands and other ships carrying away export cargoes of rails.

It will be recalled that in 1884 the passage for logs had been excavated at the portage to Lake Union. Prior to that the Lake Washington Improvement Co., headed by Judge Burke, had been organized to construct a canal for vessels of at least 3,000 tons, but nothing came of it.

Congress in 1890 appropriated $10,000 for a survey of the most feasible route. Before one could be built in a northerly direction the government would have to acquire the small log canal and Harvey Pike's old reserve.

Although six different routes for a canal had been discussed, the most strongly favored in 1892 was by way of Shilshole Bay. Gilman two years previously had been advocating this course to Salmon Bay, saying that large vessels could enter it at high tide. He became a strong advocate of building a canal there and recommended a single lock which would bring Salmon Bay and Lake Washington to the level of Lake Union. Ever the promoter, he declared, "Manufacturies, shipyards, wharves and warehouses would spring up like magic on the shores of the lake. The tracks of five transcontinental railways will touch their shores and there exchange traffic with ships from all ports of the world."

When the Democratic state convention later in the year condemned the canal proposal, Gilman was indignant, declaring the action "utterly devoid of decency and a deliberate insult to King County."

The Democrats branded the plan an expenditure of public money for the purpose of advancing private enterprises.

"Absurd," screamed an editorial in Hunt's paper.

A month later the Tacoma Ledger set out to expose the Kirkland steel works as a disguise for the proposed canal. The newspaper claimed that if the Kirkland Land Co. could get the government to dig the canal in 1893 the stockholders would become millionaires without producing an ounce of steel. They would derive all their riches from sales of land.

The Ledger charged that Hunt and his associates planned to establish another townsite at the mouth of Mercer Slough, the point on the lake nearest both the Newcastle and Gilman coal mines.

Although a bill was pending in Congress and Governor John H. McGraw had been elected on a platform of "Dig the Ditch," Tacoma succeeded in raising such strong opposition that all support of the measure was withdrawn in the national capital. Congress made one concession; it ordered a reexamination of the proposal.

In Kirkland the Democratic censure spelled doom for the town. If the mill had been a going concern, maybe the canal would have succeeded that year. But it was now too late to resuscitate the would-be metropolis, although one new industry was coming to life there.

Kirk had persuaded Edward Eyanson to move his woolen mill from Columbia City, Ind. to the Lake Washington community. The plant was erected near the foot of Market Street and stayed there until 1927. During the First World War it employed up to 250 persons.

But for the most part The Ledger was strictly truthful in describing Kirkland as "The townsite waiting for a town" and pointing to "Coal bunkers that are waiting for coal."

The woolen mill at Kirkland.

Old Picture - of Kirkland waterfront - *University of Washington Library.*

A force greater than the schemes of Daniel Gilman and Leigh Hunt was at work. Far away in London, Baring Brothers Bank had failed late in 1890 and, like a pebble dropped in a pond, ripples of the catastrophe to this international banking institution were being felt. The Pacific Northwest was experiencing tight money in 1892. A hint of what could be expected was to be seen in the defaulting by Eastern stockholders on their subscriptions to the Great Western Iron & Steel Co. These were the first twinges of the great depression that was just ahead in 1893.

At first the steel mill was able to borrow from the assets of the land company, but the latter suspended loans in December, 1893, and it was apparent the mill could not function for lack of finances. It was finally foreclosed by sheriff's sale in July, 1895.

For the next ten years Kirkland was an empty place, its new buildings tenantless. The mill equipment was left to gather rust without ever having gone into production. More than $1,000,000 was lost around Kirkland in those years of hard times.

The Lake Washington Belt Line had never been used and was torn up later. It was enjoined,

Kirkland's waterfront park in the center of the city is popular with spectators, ducks and boats. The shore beyond here to the south is lined with condominiums. *Photo by Greg Gilbert.*

Waterfront apartments line the shore south of Kirkland. *Photo by Greg Gilbert*

restrained and delayed by every possible means and so hampered and put to such costs it had to give up. (Hunt and Furth were members of its board.) Kirk and others found business opportunities elsewhere and the machinery of the mill eventually was sold, some to the Moran shipyard, which was building the battleship *Nebraska* and some to the Hofius Iron Works in Seattle.

Kirk stayed on and lived in his turreted and many-gabled wooden house until 1902. The residence remained standing nine more years, but Kirk meanwhile moved to a farm on San Juan Island. He was blamed for the catastrophic ending of the town, but he, too, had lost a fortune there.

The steel mill was Kirkland's only flurry of excitement. The town became one of Seattle's dormitory suburbs, connected with the city by ferryboats in the first years of the present century. The name of Moss Bay for its harbor was forgotten until lately. The business center moved from Market Street to Kirkland Avenue.

Before there were bridges over the lake the Kirkland ferry crossing became the most popular, being considered the end of the transcontinental highway known as the Yellowstone Trail. The former landing place is today part of a city park. Apartments now line the shore to the south of it and a different set of values prevails from the era when smokestacks and warehouses were envisioned as essential to the waterfront.

Houghton

Until 1968 Houghton and Kirkland were separate cities, the former town intensely jealous of its independence of its larger neighbor. Houghton was the older of the two and was the most important community on the East Side for a long time.

After the arrival of the Pophams and the Frenches on the lakeshore Edwin M. Church in 1875 claimed the 180 acres next north of French and J.W. DeMott selected land in what is now Kirkland's business center. Andrew Nelson and his sons homesteaded the hilly area west of Market Street and extending northward in Kirkland toward Juanita Bay. Nelson's was some of the property which Hunt and his associates bought up.

Houghton's importance was due partially to a road cut through the heavy timber from there to Redmond in 1879. This was called the Curtis Road (N.E. 52nd Street) for the Curtis family living at the boat landing. There were numerous Curtises, James having come about 1872 and homesteaded. One of his sons, Frank, did not move to the lake until 1883. He built a house for himself which became a stopping place for travelers. Curtis Landing was where the later wharves were. The road leading to it was the only overland route to the back country around and beyond Lake Sammamish.

Loggers began operating in the vicinity of the landing about 1875, among them Willard Houghton. Another was William Cochrane, who cut over the Popham property.

A store was opened when the road was hacked out and Houghton became a trading center.

A letter written in November, 1885 by Judge Everett Smith described a 10-mile tramp near Houghton "through as wild and primitive country" as the writer had ever seen. He told of crossing the lake to visit a Mr. Wells, a court bailiff who went home weekends. The boat, Smith said, made stops wherever some settler waved a blanket or an apron as a signal.

He went on to describe his walk:

"Every man has 160 acres, which puts cabins about half a mile apart. Each cabin has about it a clearing of a few acres, one to six generally. All about it is the immense forest. The few country roads are simply trails wide enough for an ox team to get through the brush.

"We followed these trails, keeping within a quarter mile of the lake and calling at several of the cabins. Five-sixths of the settlers in that section are bachelors. These poor fellows keep house, doing all their own cooking and work. During certain seasons they leave their ranches and work in the city or else in lumber camps . . . A mile or so from the lake the land is open to claims, but all bordering the lake anywhere near the city are held at fictitious values. If I had a couple of months spare time I should preempt a claim on the east side and hold it on spec."

Settlers, Smith reported, carried guns, not for defense, but to drop any game they might meet. Hunting was fine around the lake. The homesteaders shot partridge and deer.

"Venison is cheap in the market," Smith added.

Houghton was soon to become a place for building boats. The first may have been the *Squak*, constructed in 1884 by Captain J.C. O'Connor, who had taken land east of French. He bought Mrs. McGregor's north 80 acres, rebuilt her cabin, put up a dock and built two boats. Mrs. O'Connor took in travelers.

By 1904 the community had a full-fledged boatyard the Bartsch & Tompkins* Transportation Co., which consolidated three years later with the Anderson Steamboat Co. The yard was primitive, with hauling done by horse, wagon and mule-powered windlass. Equipment was stored in a single 10 by 12 foot shanty and workmen brought their own tools.

Yarrow Bay was then much larger and more navigable, so that a boat could go to Northup Landing, where is now a heavily traveled highway intersection leading to the Evergreen Point Bridge. This is the junction of Lake Washington Boulevard and State Highway 520.

The landing was named for James Northup, father of Benson L. Northup, publisher of Seattle's first (1876) city directory and a former teacher at Denny School. Benson moved to the country to engage in the seed business and selected land south of where his wife's brother, Frank Curtis was located. His father took his homestead in 1875. The son later moved to the very wildest part of the Olympic Peninsula, the Clearwater Valley.

Yarrow Bay began as Northup Bay and the name was not changed until Leigh Hunt moved to Yarrow Point.

In Northup's time husbands often worked in Seattle and rowed home weekends to see their families. This is what a neighbor, John Zwiefelhofer, did. Once he carried a 100-pound sack of flour on his back the five miles from the landing to the farm he had settled on in the valley in 1882. After the Seattle fire Zwiefelhofer made farming his full-time occupation and raised strawberries for market.

Note:

* Captain George Bartsch was captain of the first double-ended ferryboat on the lake, the *King County*. He was also master of the *Gazelle* and the *Dorothy*. His partner, Captain Harry Tompkins, spent 48 years steamboating on the lake.

Points Country and Medina

Long ago when the level of the water was higher the three points southwest of Houghton had shapes different from their present ones. Yarrow Bay had a marsh at its head and here was another place where Indians gathered wapatoes.

The next bay west, Cozy Cove, was then called Anderson Bay, for the well known steamboat captain who was later to have his shipyard nearby.

The points country attracted loggers, for the timber was readily accessible to the water. Marshall Blinn became the first private owner of Hunts Point in 1871, the year prior to his purchase of the Denny Park tract. The arm of land was called Long Point until Leigh S.J. Hunt bought it in 1888 from Blinn's heirs.

Hunt later deeded a portion to Jacob Furth and Bailey Gatzert, who were with him in some of his ventures. Furth and Hunt also owned Evergreen (then Fairweather) Point. In the same period of land speculation Hunt and C.A. Cummins bought Yarrow Point, which had been homesteaded by Wilbur W. Easter and planted partly to orchards. On its west side was a boat landing, Lucerne. Hunt

An old view of Medina from the lake. *University of Washington Library*

named the point for a place in southern Scotland mentioned in his two favorite poems by Wordsworth. Here he built a two-story home with 14-foot ceilings and resided in it until the demise of the steel mill, when he took off for North Korea and recouped his fortunes in gold mines. He paid off his debts, but never lived on Yarrow or in the vicinity of Seattle again. Some of his losses had been incurred in 1893 when a run occurred on a bank of which he was director. It kept open until panicky depositors cleaned it.

Hunt had a varied career. A graduate of the University of Michigan, he had been president of Iowa Agricultural College. He resigned that post to move to Seattle, where he accumulated considerable wealth within a few years.

In the period of his exploitation of the Kirk project Hunt, Furth and Gatzert sold Hunt's Point to H.A. Noble, who had manufactured barbed wire in Illinois before moving west to assist in organizing the Kirkland Land Co., of which he became president.

After the great depression of 1893 Hunts Point was overgrown completely with trees except for a clearing near the tip where James Brewster about 1904 purchased a summer campsite. After living a rustic tent life for two seasons he built a large home there and started the trend for country estates on the East Side.

Francis Boddy in 1892 purchased land in the middle of Hunts Point and with his three sons went into dairying and the greenhouse business. He installed a small sawmill to supply his own needs and sold a little lumber.

The year the Boddys arrived the wooded portion of Yarrow Point and the head of Yarrow Bay were being logged with oxen.

Medina was heavily timbered when the original patents for government lands were granted in the 1870's. Albert King and his brothers, all of them Civil War veterans, had an entire section consisting of Groat Point and Eastland, the area north of it. Most of the property between the Furth, Hunt and Gatzert tract at Evergreen Point and the King homesteads was owned by A.C. Anderson and Henry Webster.

After loggers removed the trees the farmers came. The first four little houses belonged to Jacob and George Baum (1889), Thomas R. Burke (1889), and Samuel Belote (1890) and M. Gigy (1890). Alexander Stewart in 1893 moved to a small place near the Overlake golf links. Joseph Croft arrived shortly after Seattle's fire.

Some of the newcomers lived in log cabins left by the men who had homesteaded the timber claims. Most took to raising strawberries.

T.L. Dabney, who was in business in Seattle, constructed the first dock and proposed calling the community Flordeline. Others did not like his choice. Mrs. Belote, Mrs. Burke and Mrs. Gigy consulted a geography for a better name and picked on Medina. A sign was painted, but Dabney one night took it down. His neighbors retaliated by getting rid of the one he substituted.

Unlike the Arabian city, the East Side Medina always has been pronounced with a long "i"; it was more easily understood that way on the telephone.

Much of the property for a long time remained idle and in the hands of absentee owners like Anderson, who controlled the present golf course and adjacent waterfront. The trend toward lakeshore estates began in 1905, the year Edward E. Webster, secretary and general manager of Seattle's Independent Telephone Co., erected "The Gables." The second large house at Medina was built by Lee DeVries, Seattle attorney. In 1909 he bought a place with an old log cabin on it and camped there summers. Later he moved to California and his residence was taken over between 1921 and 1926 for the Medina Baby Home, a branch of the Pacific Coast Rescue and Protective Society.

Captain Elias W. Johnston, who had made a fortune in the Yukon, moved to Medina about 1912, purchasing seven and a half acres on both sides of Dabney's Landing, where the lake ferryboats picked up passengers. Johnston erected a mansion with a pagoda roof and Japanese-style gate columns. Wanting to end the nuisance of a commercial boat landing so near, he arranged with King County to exchange ground for another dock site at the south end of Evergreen Point Road. Medina's city hall is in the old ferry building there.

Johnston and William C. Calvert platted a portion of Medina and conducted a realty sales campaign in 1919. Among those attracted by the large waterfront tracts were Miller Freeman, publisher, and several prominent lumbermen, William Neil Winter, James N. Clapp and James G. Eddy, all of Everett, and W.B. Nettleton, of Seattle. In the 1920s they erected the beautiful homes which in recent years were owned respectively by S.W. Thurston, Dr. Robert M. Campbell, Kemper Freeman, Langdon Simons Jr. and Norton Clapp.

The mansions are considerably changed, their water towers gone or converted to other uses and the acreage divided. There are now five homes on the Eddy estate, the owners jointly maintaining a paved driveway leading to the V-shaped wharf and large summer house.

In the same period the Overlake Golf and Country Club was organized and yachts were moored in front of the big estates. The term "gold coast" was coined and Medina rated high in the social status. Often the estates were occupied only half the year, their owners away traveling the rest of the time.

Eventually the golf club could not weather the depression and it closed in 1934. James Clapp pur-

Captain Elias W. Johnston's imposing residence built at Medina about 1912. It had a pagoda roof and Japanese style gate columns. *University of Washington Library.*

chased the 160-acre tract and turned it into Fairways Farm, where he and his wife bred Arabian and Palomino horses. The club house was dismantled and a long white barn with gabled roof arose in its place.

The farm was in addition to Clapp's Lakelure estate, consisting of a French colonial house surrounded by 10 acres of woodland and formal gardens. In 1943 Clapp moved to another ranch he owned in California and sold his residence to Gilbert W. Skinner and Fairways to Neil Jamison.

A year later Clapp was killed when a tractor overturned on him. His half-brother, Norton Clapp, president of the Weyerhaeuser Co., was a later arrival in Medina, buying the Nettleton house after it was for a number of years the country home of C.B. Blethen, publisher of the Seattle Times.

As for the golf course, Jamison ran Hereford cattle on it until it was sold again. In 1952 it was leased to the reorganized Overlake Club, which has occupied the property ever since.

Incorporation of Medina was proposed when the Mercer Island Floating Bridge opened. An improvement club was organized in 1923 and became a clearing house for discussion of civic betterment. However, the municipality was not formed until 1955.

Medina is zoned only for residential property and, if its store had not been in the same building more than 50 years, it would be out of business. The owner, though a city councilman, could not obtain a building permit for exterior alterations, therefore the modern food mart appears about as it was when George Tapp opened it around 1910 and the community's second wedding was held in the hall upstairs.

Medina extends from the tip of Evergreen Point south to Dabney Point, Groat Point and Meydenbauer Bay. It lies along the Lake Washington shore west of Clyde Hill and Bellevue and has a population of probably 3,000.

The Evergreen Point Bridge approach cuts through the northern portion of the community, separating one of Medina's two parks from the main section of town. Evergreen Point Road, undisturbed by the freeway, crosses it on an overpass near the former toll plaza.

One of the peculiarities of the town is that its estates have better streets than those belonging to the city. Evergreen Point Road, the main thoroughfare, terminates in two dead ends. It was paved in 1917 and the date was marked on it.

Medina's city hall is a former ferryboat terminal. *Greg Gilbert photo.*

Bellevue's Beginning and Beaux Arts

Much of the timber in Medina and Bellevue was logged by Isaac Bechtel, Sr., who arrived in 1882 from Ontario, Canada. With the help of his sons he commenced cutting five years later, employing six teams and running a track with wooden rails through what is now the shopping square. Another tram road went into the old Bellevue cemetery on 116th Street. The trams had eight wheels and the youngest son remembered when he was 13 being employed to go along and grease the skids.

Meydenbauer Bay at that time often was so full of logs a skilled man could walk across on them.

The elder Bechtel was killed in 1890 while working alone unloading a tram car at Wildwood on the bay.

Need for a school among the homestead families brought about their first common endeavor. Albert S. Burrows in 1882 took a mile and a quarter of lake frontage at Killarney, on the south side of Bellevue, land he had been shown by another settler, George

First Postmistress in Bellevue Mrs. Bechtel,

M. Miller. The latter lived at Beaux Arts and wanted to have a family nearby so that the children of the two households would justify maintaining a school.

The two fathers towed a raft of lumber six miles from the Guy Phinney mill on the west side of the lake and built a 12-by-12 foot shanty of upright boards on Burrows' land for the school. Its blackboard consisted of three 12-inch boards four feet long. The three home-made seats accommodated two children each. The fathers also made a desk for the teacher, who was Burrows' oldest daughter, Calanthia Wyomia.

The next year Charles Olds and family, with two children, moved to the east side of Mercer Island to another piece of property Miller had helped find. Miller made a business of locating claims for settlers and was paid for his services.

Meanwhile in 1882 a newcomer, Patrick Downey, built a log cabin in heavily timbered Vuecrest, where he was later to become a prosperous strawberry farmer. He named Clyde Landing, north of Bellevue on Meydenbauer Bay, for some association with the River Clyde in Scotland. The name has survived in present Clyde Hill.

Downey and Miller agreed that the school might as well be moved to a homestead shanty on the property of Miller's son on Mercer Island, where the present state highway approaches the East Channel Bridge. They thought the Bellevue children old enough to row across to it.

Burrows opposed the plan, so it was decided to divide the school term, holding it two months on the island and two months on the mainland.

Olds' daughter recalled, "Mr. Burrows was so angry he wouldn't let his children attend that fall. He didn't think it safe for them to cross the water."

If the new teacher hadn't boarded with the Olds, it is doubtful that winter if their children would have gone to school either.

Near the head of Meydenbauer Bay in 1900. The white building is the school built in 1892 up the hill from the boat landing at Bellevue. *Photo Seattle Historical Society.*

Whaling Fleet in Meydenbauer Bay *Williams S. Lagen collection*

"The teacher did not know much about rowing," explained Alla Olds Luckenbill. "One November day the boat swamped, we were soaked and Father had to rescue us. Mother was so worried she wouldn't let us go by boat any more in bad weather. In the end the teacher moved to the school and batched and the Millers were the only pupils attending the second month. The water was calm opposite their house (at Beaux Arts) and they didn't mind rowing.

"When the remaining months of school were held on the Bellevue side, we didn't go. Mother taught us for five years. Sometimes we had a tutor."

Attendance in Bellevue increased to nine children when in 1886 the school made another move to the Downey property, occupying a shake shanty in a berry field north of the present Catholic Church. Next a one-room building, 16-by 20 feet in dimensions, was erected on Main Street. By 1892 the population had grown rapidly and the school was replaced with a larger one which stood until December, 1965. It became the high school between 1923 and 1930, then it was rented for the city hall and finally as the Veterans of Foreign Wars clubhouse.

Mathew S. Sharpe was Bellevue's first postmaster, beginning July 21, 1886. Prior to that he had carried the mail from Houghton for his neighbors. Sharpe served less than a year, dying at the age of 31. He and his brothers, Lucian and James, had moved there in 1882 from Bellevue, Ind. and taken homesteads totalling 640 acres on what is now the business district. When it came to giving the new post office a name Matt Sharpe argued in favor of borrowing from his former home town, citing the beautiful surroundings as making it appropriate.

Bellevue was not platted until 1904. It became a center of strawberry growing and retained a rural aspect until the first Lake Washington Bridge was built. The first portion platted was Moorland, south of Meydenbauer Bay.

A 1913 promotion booklet gave the population of the entire district as about 1,900. It had three stores, three elementary schools, one high school, two churches, a blacksmith shop, sawmill and shingle mill, "plenty of pure air, abundance of pure water, but no saloons."

The district largely consisted of two-to-ten acre tracts with orchards and berries. Greenhouses were common and growing flowers and vegetables for Seattle was a regular business.

After lowering of the lake in 1919 Bellevue became the home port of the American Pacific Whaling Co. fleet, which wintered six or seven

Wildwood Park, at Bellevue. *University of Washington Library*

stubby steamers each year in Meydenbauer Bay, a few hundred feet north of the yacht club. The boats operated in Alaska.

William Schupp, head of the company, had a home overlooking the wharf. The ferry from Leschi came in at another dock east of the property and beyond that was a dance hall and Wildwood Park. A large structure in the park later became a skating rink.

Schupp purchased this tract also, landscaped it and converted the rink into a house which he never completed. He sold the park after Pearl Harbor and the mansion he had started became the Meydenbauer Bay Yacht Club.

The next house beyond the park had belonged to a Captain Meagher, who commanded a tugboat which he brought into the bay. He used to empty the ash from his boilers there and great piles of it were on the beach. Schupp bought the Meagher house for members of his family to live in. Schupp died in 1948, but his descendants remain on the old property and own the marina where the whaling station was.

The only time whalers were active in Bellevue was in spring when they were fitting out and in the fall when they were storing lines and putting gear in lockers. A general overhauling went on, but there was no drydocking at Bellevue; the boats went to Houghton for that. They were away each year from the first week in May to late September.

During the Second World War the Coast Guard took over the whaling station for the inshore patrol and maintained the only barrack that was ever there.

For years a bridge spanned the marsh at the extreme end of Meydenbauer Bay, once heavily populated by bull frogs that made a thundering noise at night.

Another aspect of the waterfront was the founding of the village of Beaux Arts. Sidney Laurence, an artist famed for his Alaskan landscapes, organized the Beaux Arts Society in Seattle in 1908. Several of its members, Alfred T. Renfro, cartoonist; Frank Calvert, journalist and Finn T. Forlich, sculptor, incorporated and laid out a community on the shore north of the East Channel Bridge. The tract consisted of 50 acres and has been described as a do-it-yourself project. Ten acres were reserved in the center for joint artistic endeavor. There were to be studios and workshops for woodworking, sculpture, typography, tapestry, photography, engraving and wrought-iron designing. Several houses went up, a well was dug and a gasoline pump installed to connect with wooden pipe lines. At first the only lighting was by oil lamps and candles. Telephone messages had to be carried from Leschi. The only grocery was at Midlakes except for a floating store on a powered scow called the Grubstake, which sailed along shore once a week.

The art colony, modelled after English garden villages, failed to come up to expectations and as time went on other residents moved in. Now Beaux Arts is one of several separate little municipalities strung along the East Side, undistinguishable from Bellevue which partially surrounds it, and dependent on its larger neighbor for most public services, which are rented. The total population is less than 400. The oldest house, built in 1909, still is occupied.

Beyond the East Channel Bridge is Enatai Beach Park, so named from a Chinook jargon word meaning "across," "beyond" or "on the other side." It formerly was a boat landing called Hertford by Judge Robert Brook Albertson for his birthplace in Virginia. He owned the 48 acres to the east and permitted relatives to erect several summer homes on the property beginning in 1915. A right-of-way was bought through it when a wooden bridge to Mercer Island was completed in 1922 and at least one of the houses had to be removed from the property.

The Bellevue Ferry Landing in 1914. Photo by James P. Lee. *University of Washington Library.*

Mercer Slough

This tour of the lakeshore has arrived at the mouth of Mercer Slough, a body of water which almost has disappeared. Highway 504 runs up the slough, Bellevue's city hall and public library are built on its former shore, a nature park, blueberry farms and an industrial park fill its basin.

One must imagine the slough as it was in Aaron Mercer's day when the water of Lake Washington was nearly nine feet higher and the swamps extended on either side of the channel, which was navigable to small sternwheelers. They went inland as far as the public library. In this area was the logging community of Wilburton and its mill pond. Farther up the slough, in the depression north of Bellevue's Main Street, were beaver dams. A trapper living there one year took out 130 mink, four otter and a quantity of muskrats.

The mill at Wilburton began operating in January, 1904, having been moved from Tokul Creek, near Snoqualmie. The company was organized by eight men with logging experience who were influenced in choosing the site because Wilbur & England had a logging camp near there. The sawmill and planing mill stood southwest of the intersection of Main Street and 116th Avenue S.E.

Hard times brought misfortunes to the organizers of the mill and Wade Hewitt, one of the partners was forced to foreclose the mortgage he held. After that the company was known as Hewitt Lee Lumber Co. When the lake was lowered it had to suspend operations and sued King County for damages because of being deprived of means of transportation for its products. After losing the case in a lower court the company won in the Supreme Court and was awarded damages.

A nostalgic picture of the slough long ago was conjured up by an old Seattle resident. When he was in the seventh grade at Rainier School he and a pal frequently trolled for trout. One Saturday they ventured across from Leschi to explore Mercer Slough.

He recalled, "We traveled through cattails, tules, lily pads and several species of marsh grass and in some places had to push the canoe across shallow spots. Other places the water was four or five feet deep and it was in these spots we found several muskrat houses. Near the north end of the marsh we found a beaver house.

"That winter we trapped at Columbia City, which must have been about where Atlantic City is now. We knew the feeding places of the muskrats by the gnawed roots they brought up and left on floating pieces of driftwood and logs. We fastened our traps at these haul-ups and, when the rat was caught, it jumped in the water and drowned immediately.

"We went to Mercer Slough only on Saturdays and set our traps, returning on Sundays to check them. We had to make our haul-ups on Mercer Slough, using old pieces of wood we brought from Columbia Slough, anchored with weights and copper wire and baited with carrots and bits of apple.

"We caught as many as 300 muskrats a year. Some brought $2.25 each. We caught a few mink besides.

"Mercer Slough was such a wonderful place we went back to it in summer and camped, fishing for trout and keeping a record of the water fowl we saw. Once a green heron was caught in one of our traps and I mounted the bird and gave it to our high school. Hundreds of ducks and geese stopped at Mercer Slough; it was the finest part of the lake."

Although a maze of highway support pillars now crosses the mouth of the slough, a strong sentiment exists for saving the portion that remains. The State Parks and Recreation Commission plans to develop 520 acres and create nature trails, ponds and habitat for waterfowl.

Bellevue owns 48 acres where Boy Scouts and others helped establish Bellefields Park. Improvements were made by hand labor in order to disturb the wild inhabitants as little as possible.

The slough is fed by Kelsey and Mercer Creeks, both salmon spawning streams. In 1926 farmers formed a drainage district and dug a canal through the swamp, draining it for blueberry and vegetable farms. The canal accounts for what remains of the slough. That the area hasn't been built up is largely due to the land being peat bog, 100 feet deep in spots. The peat floats on underground water.

Factoria

Developers of shore properties and view hillside just south of Highway 90 would exclaim in horror at the suggestion that this was once considered as strictly an area for heavy industries. The hoped-for day when coal smoke would pour out of hundreds of smokestacks south and east of the East Channel Bridge never arrived.

The coal was there, it is true, a few miles back in the valleys. But names such as Coal Creek and Factoria now seem highly inappropriate.

Yet there was a day, February 9, 1910, when the first shovel of earth was moved by Mayor Hiram Gill of Seattle for the initial manufacturing plant, the Factoria Stove & Range Co., launched with a great fanfare of publicity. A Congressman was the featured speaker. A special steamship brought a crowd from Leschi. A prize of a $500 lot—in the swamp—was awarded Mrs. C.E. Douglas for naming the mythical manufacturing center.

Announcement was made that the stove plant

Factoria when it was visualized as a lake port. *University of Washington Library.*

would be in operation within two months and was to employ 100 men. The output already was signed up for a year and it was predicted the firm would be struggling to meet the great demand for its products. Real estate salesmen were busy selling lots and the manager of the Appleton Investment Co. declared that the town would be built at once. He intimated that more than 20 other manufacturing plants were planned; this would be a big city.

The publicity spree lasted only a short time. No one remembers if the stove factory ever turned out so much as one stove.

Another of the forgotton schemes for industrial development is revealed in a prospectus of the Seattle & Eastern Railway, prepared in November, 1911. It planned a passenger terminal for Medina, describing it as "five and a half miles northwest of Factoria, our proposed freight terminal which is now being successfully exploited as a manufacturing center."

The prospectus stated that timber was then being logged between Factoria and Issaquah and as the land was very productive it would be developed for truck farming and fruit raising. Issaquah was expected to reach a population of 5,000. The Issaquah, Superior and Grand Ridge coal mines were operating and another of the U.S. Coal Co. four miles up the hill would shortly be in production.

"The railroad," said the prospectus, "has an option on 1,600 feet of deep-water frontage for all ocean-going vessels and 80 acres of level land for yards and warehouses. It will establish a barge and tug line and buy the Anderson Steamboat Co., Birch and Anderson Towboat Co. and the Anderson and Tompkins Truck Line and construct a new ferry to run from Leschi to Medina."

The company planned to build a standard gauge railway from Factoria to Issaquah and a branch line of lighter construction for passenger traffic to connect with the ferry, also two spurs to the coal mines. Nothing ever came of this ambitious program and Factoria was dormant until a shopping center opened there near Highway 405 in the 1970s.

Newcastle: the Coal Mine Story Continued

Newport, where yachts today anchor in basins beside their owner's homes, was another "paper" town of the same period. At the turn of the century it was nothing but submerged marsh and vacant land adjoining the farm August Havercamp had acquired in 1887 at the mouth of Coal Creek.

Much of the waste carried downstream from the coal mines was deposited on Havercamp's property. Although he sold some coal, he once got a judgment against the mining company for ruining the creek where it passed through his land.

The thriving mining region known as Newcastle is today reduced to a ruined bunker and a couple of old houses. The slag heaps are overgrown and there is nothing to indicate the former extent and importance of the industry.

To resume the story of these mines, the Seattle Coal & Transportation Co. sold out in 1880 to the Henry Villard interests and merged into the Oregon Improvement Co. During a depression four years later, development of coal mining and shipping on

A ruined bunker is Newcastle's principal landmark today. *Photo by Greg Gilbert*

a large scale was a stabilizing factor in Seattle's economy. Coal went to the financial rescue of the city after the fire of 1889, when bunkers and wharves figured in the initial construction following the conflagration.

The year preceding the fire was marked by labor troubles at Newcastle. In December, 1888 friction flared between the company and employees who joined the Miners' Union and the Knights of Labor. Riots followed and arms were shipped in January to 50 striking miners. The company requested protection of the militia, charging that the sheriff and his deputies were members of the Knights of Labor and would do nothing to prevent trouble. Before the disturbance ended one man was killed by a rifle shot.

By 1893 more coal was taken from the high-grade lignite deposit at Newcastle than from any other mine in Washington up to that year. The upper three levels had been abandoned because of fires from spontaneous combustion. The mine was extremely dry in the bottom and, to avoid dust explosions, gangways had to be kept wet continuously.

On October 9, 1894 shifts were changing in mid-afternoon and miners were in the gangways. On the fifth level, 2,000 feet below the surface, 127 men were scattered along 4,000 feet of tunnel. Suddenly a ball of fire shot 600 feet down the corridor, followed by stifling smoke.

The injured lay, faces buried in coal dust, beside the dead mules which had been used to pull mine cars. Among the victims were two boys, 15 and 16. Four men were burned fatally and five others were in serious condition.

The following December 17 another holocaust occurred. The mine was a seething furnace and men on the lower levels could escape only through air shafts, pulling themselves up with a rope where no steps existed. This time all were accounted for and when they had reached safety the mine was flooded. Workers dammed Coal Creek with a wall of baled hay, brush and dirt and turned the stream into a hastily cleared ditch leading to the mine. Clouds of smoke and steam hung over the slope for

Newcastle - These were some of the mine buildings at Coal Creek. *Seattle Times photo from collecion of Miss Elizabeth Greggs.*

days. No more mining could be done until new slopes were opened and this threw more than 160 men out of employment.

The company's older mine at Newcastle proper by then was producing only inferior coal, burned in company engines. At the time of the fire the principal mine had been at the community of Coal Creek, a mile and a half away. After the disaster the deposit had to be worked from other points.

A new slope was sunk inside the town limits of old Newcastle in 1895 by the Pacific Coast Co., which purchased the property. By 1924 the seams had been worked out and many miners went away.

The town of Newcastle in its heyday had 200 houses and Coal Creek had 300 inhabitants. They were mostly English, Welsh, Finnish, Scotch and Irish. A Chinese crew picked reject coal from the bunkers. Many young boys were employed underground as unskilled labor. One told of earning 8½ cents an hour as trap boy, opening and closing doors in gangways to let the mule cars through. He worked a ten-hour day. He had been employed a week when the first explosion occurred and he was laid up two months with severe burns about his face, neck and hands. He was back at work by the time of the December fire, greasing mine cars on the surface, so missed injury in that disaster.

Among this miner's boyhood memories was his first Fourth of July. He had recently arrived from Wales and knew nothing about the holiday, which was celebrated at Newcastle in most rugged fashion. The miners' concept of fireworks was to take sticks of dynamite to the slag heap and detonate them.

Another of his recollections was of a trip to Seattle when he missed a train to Newcastle on a Sunday. In order to get home in time for work he rode a Seattle, Rainier & Southern streetcar to Renton, arrived there at 9 p.m., borrowed a lantern from a shoemaker and walked six miles to Newcastle, sometimes on a trestle, six stories high, across May Creek valley.

Newcastle Landing was just north of Pleasure Point where homes now line the waterfront. This area also is known as Lake Lanes and is remembered by oldtimers as a picnic spot.

Logging and grading have obliterated all traces of the coal period; not even so much as bits of the black mineral turn up.

Several families lived at the landing in the early period, the men tending the bunkers. Both workmen and scattered farmers had to go to Newcastle for their mail, climbing the steep hill, following the tram line and crossing gullies on its trestles.

After the old route was abandoned new bunkers for Newcastle coal were erected at about S.E. 110th Street in Renton and a wharf extended out from the present Boeing property. Marshes lay between the bunkers and the dock, crossed by trestles of the Columbia and Puget Sound Railway.

Trestle on the early coal route, Columbia River and Puget Sound Railroad.

Mercer Island

Mercer Island was a wild place of doubtful agricultural value when Vitus Schmidt went there about 1876. He was a German wagonmaker from Baden who had come to the United States at 15 after serving his apprenticeship. He worked his way west, building snowsheds for the Northern Pacific Railroad.

Arriving in Seattle, he took a land claim on the east shore of Mercer Island with John Wenzler, another German who was a shoemaker, and they built a log cabin. One day they were clearing land when a wind storm toppled a large fir on their house, completely demolishing it. This discouraged them and they left their land claim.

Schmidt went East, married and had two children. Hard times overtook him and he returned to Seattle. After a while he filed on another homestead on the island. He moved back to it in 1889 after his first wife had died and he remarried.

Meanwhile the island had acquired some other families, the Gardiner Proctors, south of the present floating bridge, and Charles Olds with his wife and children on the East Channel side.

Olds named his place Appleton because he planted an orchard on it. Some of his old trees may still be there, varieties like Ben Davis and Twenty-Ounce Pippins, which the present generation would be at a loss to identify.

Schmidt donated an acre for a school, which stood where the Mercer Island Library now is. The school was open only five years, then so many families moved away there were not enough children to justify it.

Logging on the island ended about 1900. Second growth came up rapidly and the woods were full of deer, grouse and other game. Hunters became such a nuisance that a state law was passed making it a misdemeanor to hunt on any island in a Washington lake.

As earlier land owners moved away activity centered around East Seattle, where C.C. Calkins purchased the Proctor claim and additional property in 1889.

Calkins had landed in Seattle two years earlier with $300 in his pocket and in ten days owned 21,000 acres and was $19,000 in debt. He sold 700 acres within a few days, wiped out his debts and retained land said to have been worth $170,000 at boom prices.

He promoted "an extensive floral and residence park" on the island, guaranteeing home owners and guests at his hotel a five-cent fare to the city, including rides on the cable railroad and a lake steamer. He operated a boat, the *C.C. Calkins*, to accommodate his patrons.

Here is a newspaper advertisement from those happy days:

Why.
It's the talk
of
the town!
What is?
Why the future of East Seattle.
They say it is going to be the
Coney Island of Washington Territory.
Everybody and his best girl were out
sailing and on the island Sunday.
The cable cars were crowded, the lake
was alive with steam craft and pleasure
boats of all descriptions.

Prior to 1901 the island had only four inhabited places—the Olds property, the Lucas-Schmidt community, the William P. Guitteau house and East Seattle. Trading was done in Seattle and groceries were carried on backs to the Yesler cable cars in gunny sacks, sugar or flour sacks. The farmers on reaching the lake either boarded their own small boats or else took the *Calkins* and walked the rest of the way home.

The island had many overgrown skid roads, with here and there remains of temporary logging structures such as bunkhouses, cookhouses and sheds for horses. It had been the custom after an area was logged for the camp to move on scows to the next place. Only a year or so was necessary for the skid roads to become overgrown and impassable. The logs rotted fast and devil's club, blackberry vines, and red huckleberries speedily took possession.

Calkins had two properties on the island, East Seattle and what he planned as his own homesite, where later Luther Burbank School stood facing the East Channel south of Calkins Point (now Burbank County Park.) Prior to his acquiring the site this place was known as Guitteau's Landing. Guitteau had acquired five acres there from Calkins in 1888. He was hired by Calkins to lay out a passable road

C.C. Calkins' hotel on Mercer Island, 1890. *University of Washington Library*

Another view of East Seattle. *University of Washington Library*

The dock at East Seattle, where the hotel was located. *University of Washington Library*

across the island connecting his employer's two developments.

Calkins erected a large house and surrounded it with extensive plantings. He had a barn and two smaller buildings; one of them, a six-sided potting shed with a reservoir. He also built a bird house that was a miniature copy of his turreted hotel. The house burned but some of the buildings escaped the fire.

About 1902 Calkins sold his East Seattle Hotel. It went through several ownerships and stood empty at times. A description at the peak of its popularity in 1891 tells of walks, mazes, flowers, more than 12,000 trees, a greenhouse, 635 varieties of roses, 25 fountains, 25 arc lights mounted on 80-foot towers, a boat house for 100 boats, Turkish baths, a waterfront boulevard and 28 dressing rooms for bathers.

Eugene Lawson bought the hotel after Calkins failed. Later Major Cicero Newell took it over and made it into a school for delinquent boys. He gave it up and the Seattle School Board purchased ten acres

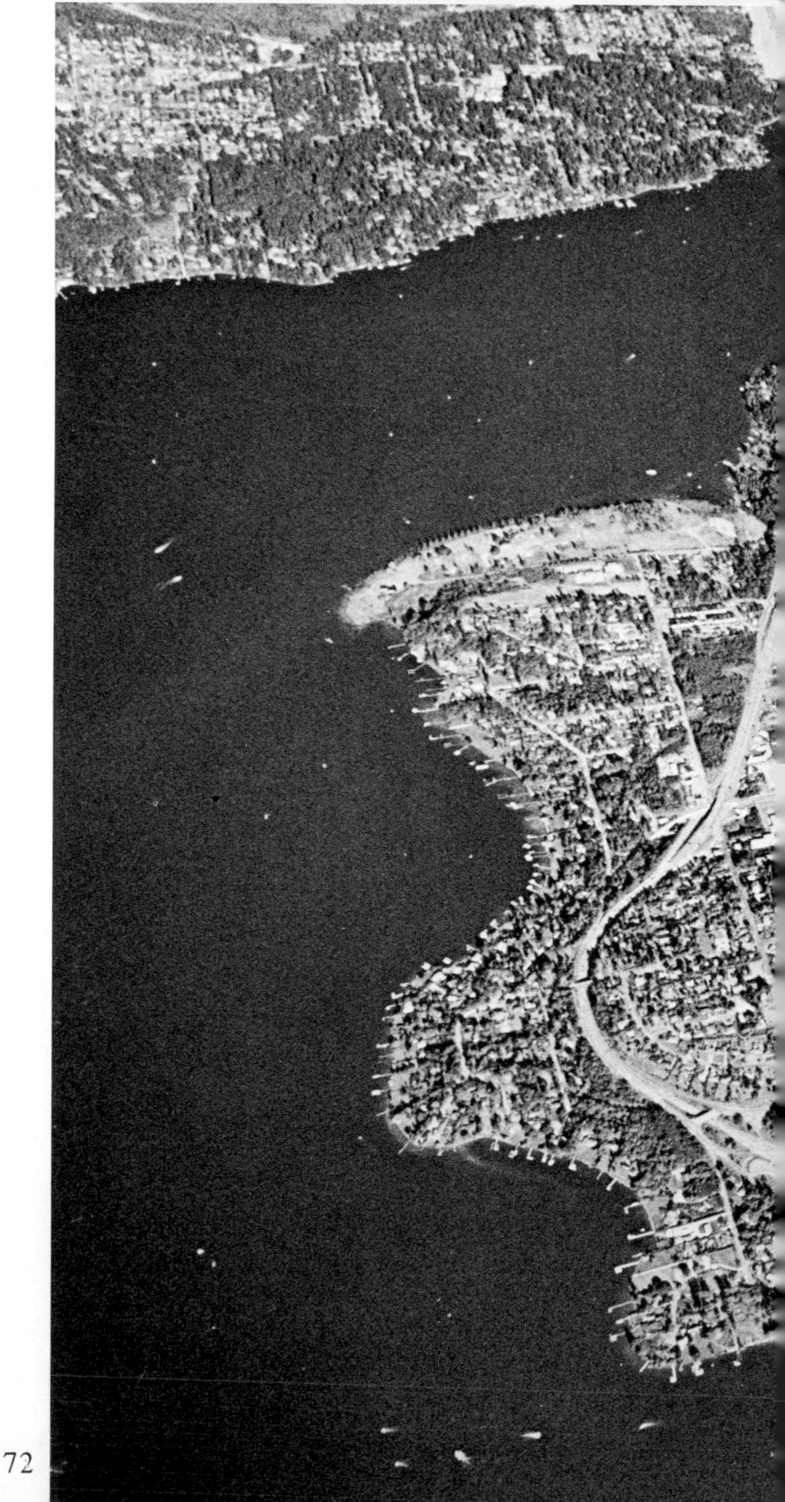

Aerial view of Mercer Island. Beaux Arts is to upper right of the small East Channel Bridge. *Photo by Greg Gilbert*

Fortuna Park was just a picnic spot on the east side of the island, north of the East Channel Bridge. *University of Washington Library*

of Calkins' property on the east shore for an industrial, or parental, school, opened in 1905 as the Luther Burbank School. Seattle was one of the few places in the nation maintaining such a service. The Martha Washington School on the city side of the lake near Seward Park was the girls' equivalent.

When the boys were gone from Calkins' hotel a doctor was the next owner. He equipped it as a sanatorium and place for curing alcoholics. Then a woman took over and ran it as a boarding house.

The doctor was back again when in the summer of 1908 the place went up in flames. A Japanese houseboy had resented a scolding and, to get even, plugged a chimney with greasy rags to create a big smoke. Instead the place caught on fire and burned like tinder.

When automobiles came into use Mercer Island had extremely poor roads and no way for cars to leave because the lake ferries were not built to accommodate them. Residents declared that a bridge to the mainland was a necessity and the logical place for it was across the narrow East Channel at Enatai. Their pleas prevailed and in the summer of 1923 work was started on a long wooden trestle. It extended 1,200 feet but was only 20 feet in width. A swing truss span in the center was almost never opened for boats because someone had to be sent to turn the wheel manually.

After a one-mile stretch of road was improved to connect with Lake Washington Boulevard island residents were able to drive to Seattle by way of Renton. More than a score of years were yet to pass before they could reach the mainland in a car by any other route.

About 22,000 persons live today on Mercer Island, which is a separate municipality with a thriving business district, supermarkets, schools, library, country club and beach club. Numerous apartments have risen in the north end, among them the Shorewood development, which includes old Fortuna Park, once a popular recreation and picnic spot. The place of the latter has been taken by Luther Burbank County Park, an 80-acre site with 4,000 feet of waterfront, a boat moorage, fishing pier and extensive recreational facilities.

Colman house - From the windows of this house at Kennydale Mrs. James Manning Colman watched her husband leave in a rowboat the day he disappeared. Long the oldest home on the east side of the lake (built about 1877), it is now gone. The picture was taken in 1955 when Mrs. Colman still lived there. *Seattle Times photo*

The Colman Murder Mystery

On a slope overlooking Lake Washington Boulevard south of the tip of Mercer Island and near May Creek at Kennydale used to stand one of the East Side's oldest houses, reminder of an unsolved mystery of pioneer days.

A series of legal procedures resulted in which the defendant, one historian observed, "had the remarkable experience of being tried more energetically, more frequently and at more different places, before more different judges and jurors than any other person in the criminal annals of the territory or state."

Coleman Point is named for the murder victim. Mapmakers erred in their spelling (as they did at Northup landing) and gave Janes Manning Colman an extra "e" in his name.

Colman's family comprised the only inhabitants of that part of the shore and his place often was a stopping point for persons en route to Newcastle. The farmer was a native of Kentucky and a descendant of Mayflower stock. He had been a Georgia legislator before moving to Washington Territory in the fall of 1875 and purchasing the 100-acre Sullivan homestead. Only one acre was cleared

when he moved there with his wife, Clara, and four children. He took active part in local affairs and was elected county commissioner in 1880 and again in 1882.

Illegal procurement of titles to public lands was a frequent practice in that day and one which Colman stoutly opposed. He became suspicious of the circumstances surrounding the claim which George M. Miller of Beaux Arts had encouraged his son, John, to acquire on Mercer Island.

Colman contended that he could prove the youth was under age by producing records of a school which the children of both families attended at Newcastle Landing. This evidently was several years after the boating disagreements related to the school on John Miller's property near the present East Channel Bridge. It was alleged in the subsequent trouble that Miller, meeting Colman, threatened to shoot the latter if he ever testified adversely about the boy's age.

Colman persisted in his charge and both men were subpoenaed to appear before a grand jury in Seattle at 10 a.m. Monday, February 8, 1886.

On the preceding day a 16-year-old lad, Wilbur Patten, rowed from Seattle with a friend, Walter Wilson. The Colmans invited the visiting boy to stay overnight, saying he could return to Seattle when the farmer went to court.

At 6:30 a.m. Monday Colman and Wilbur got into the rowboat. Mrs. Colman and her daughter watched from a livingroom window until the craft was hidden from sight by the south tip of Mercer Island. That was the last time she saw her husband alive.

Meanwhile Miller arrived alone at the courthouse slightly later than scheduled. No witness appeared against him, nor were any school records submitted. He returned home and nothing apparently was thought of Colman's absence. Seattle had plenty on its calendar that critical week, for the anti-Chinese riots were at their peak.

However, Wilbur's sister wondered about his failure to return and the friend at whose home he lived walked out to John Mathiesen's home in the Brighton area to inquire. There he learned from Matthiesen's son about the boat trip to May Creek and was satisfied that the boy was still visiting across the lake.

John Matthiesen meanwhile was absent that day at Newcastle selling vegetables to the miners. On his return trip he passed Mrs. Colman's and she told him her husband was not yet home.

The Colman house looked toward the south point of Mercer Island, scene of the murder. The house site now is overgrown with brush. *Photo by Greg Gilbert*

When Matthiesen got back and heard of the query about Wilbur he suspected something was wrong. He rowed across the lake to find out more from Mrs. Colman. She concluded immediately that her husband must have been killed. It developed that Mrs. Matthiesen had heard shots early Monday morning. Matthiesen organized a search, but not until February 12 was Colman's boat found near an unoccupied house on the west side of Mercer Island, almost directly opposite the Matthiesen home. Traces of blood were on the seats.

Two men, hastening to notify Sheriff John J. McGraw, found him with the militia companies that were lined up to hear Governor Watson Squire formally thank the troops for their services during the anti-Chinese trouble.

Suspicion for the crime immediately fell upon Miller because of the bad feeling between the two families. The sheriff went with a posse that night to Miller's home to arrest him. John was absent in Newcastle looking for a job, but he went to Seattle and gave himself up the next day.

Search for the bodies continued and they were found March 15 in 15 feet of water three miles south of where the boat was beached. Colman's watch and money were gone and this caused some persons to believe the crime was the work of Indians.

Each body bore two bullet wounds from a .40-60 Winchester fired from two different sides, as though the assailant was first in ambush and then in a boat.

Miller owned such a rifle, but when the sheriff returned to look for it and arrest Miller a second time, the weapon had vanished.

McGraw took his prisoner to see the bodies.

"There," exclaimed the sheriff, "how do you feel in the presence of your hellish crime?"

Miller, a slow-witted, country fellow, looked away and breathed hard. He had dully maintained his innocence in the face of the sheriff's hostile and threatening attitude.

Much circumstantial evidence was marshalled against Miller. One of the witnesses was nine-year-old Alla Olds, who had seen a black boat like Miller's being rowed north from the direction of the crime that fateful morning. A woman appeared to be at the oars. It was immediately assumed that she was Miller's eldest daughter, Lizzie.

Miller was indicted for both murders. To ensure a fair trial the case was taken to Port Townsend. After being out 40 hours the jury failed to agree and a second trial was held in April, 1887 in Seattle. This jury, out two days and nights, also failed to reach a verdict. In June a jury of Kitsap County citizens found Miller guilty and he was sentenced to be hanged September 23,

When asked by the judge if he had anything to say for himself he replied only, "I had nothing to do with the crime charged."

A stay of execution was granted by the governor and in February, 1888 the Supreme Court in a lengthy opinion held that "the verdict must have been rendered upon suspicion and passion only and not from deliberate weighing in the scales of reason."

A new trial jury was empaneled at Port Madison the next April, but the defense moved for nonsuit, which the judge granted for lack of sufficient evidence to convict. Miller went home, most of his savings dissipated in his long court battle, which had cost King County $18,000. Neighbors had taken to referring to him as "Pirate" Miller and during the extended litigation someone had burned his daughter Lizzie's house and fence. There was no question but that the man had been judged a renegade by the persons among whom he lived. His last years were sad. He suffered a paralytic stroke and died in 1893. His grave lies under the highway near the lake in Beaux Arts.

Many years later a Winchester .40-60 came to light, hidden in an old barn that was being razed at Wilburton. No one ever claimed it.

Kennydale's Later Years

As to Kennydale's later years, the place was named for Frank Kenny, brother-in-law of C.D. Hillman, a developer who purchased acreage and platted the Garden of Eden tract on part of the Colman property. Another 25 acres of this pioneer farm was sold early in the present century for a sawmill and a creosote plant for treating piling against the erosion of teredos and decay.

Thirty years ago in order to find Kennydale on a marine chart one would have had to look for Port Quendall. Once a bill of lading from England was received at Seattle calling for delivery of a creosote cargo to Port Quelland, U.S.A. Sailing instructions failed to disclose a place of that name, but it was readily identified as the plant at Kennydale.

The small industrial complex there included the Barbee Mill Co., Reilly Tar and Chemical Corp. and the J.H. Baxter & Co. piling plant. A product of the last firm was telephone poles, which were run through a lathe-like machine to remove tree bark, then stacked eight months for drying before being drilled and notched to suit the purchaser. As a final step they were treated with an infusion of pentachlorophenal to increase the wood's resistance to weathering.

The sawmill and Baxter's are still in the business but the Reilly plant was discontinued a few years ago. It was on the spot so long that oil and tar soaked into the ground to a depth of 45 feet.

Barbee Mill Co. *Photo by Greg Gilbert*

At the end of the Second World War a large number of surplus Navy vessels such as barges and Liberty ships were moored between the Barbee mill and Shuffleton. After these were gone log booms were made up there. These have disappeared lately because they interfered with a park on the beach which the City of Renton acquired.

Making up log rafts used to be a common sight not only at Kennydale and Shuffleton, but at Kenmore and Newport. Until very recent years they were regularly towed out to mills on the ship canal.

Log storage booms. Now there are not so many in the Kennydale area. *Photo by Greg Gilbert*

Resort at Renton · W.P. Smith's farm and garden resort at Renton were sketched in 1882 by an artist for West Shore Magazine. *Photo from Seattle Times.*

Early Days in Renton

With the coming of rails to Renton and Newcastle the coal moved out with greater ease, but travel accommodations for a long time remained primitive. The line was narrow-gauge and boasted a solitary passenger coach.

A month before the rails reached Newcastle Charles K. Jenner, who had been teaching there, was hired to take over the Renton school for the customary short term lasting two to three months. With his family he set out in January, 1877 over the old route by coal tram to Newcastle Landing, walking from there to May Creek and rowing from the Colman farm to Black River Landing.

"The road from Black River was poorly defined," his daughter recalled. "It was a dark rainy evening, the mud was thick and the Colman boy had to go ahead of us with a lantern.

"We were relieved at last to see a glimmering light. It was at Smith's Gardens, the one nursery near Seattle. A pretty little Englishwoman welcomed us, built a huge fire to dry us out and gave us tea, toast, butter and jelly."

A few years later W.P. Smith's place was described in West Shore magazine as "a very handsome pleasure garden" where Seattleites went for picnics. The farmer took in paying guests overnight and raised dairy products to sell to miners. Smith's land lay east of Williams Street and north of Liberty Park.

When the Jenner family arrived the Renton mine had closed. The teacher moved into a large structure which had been a miners' boarding house facing Cedar River. The house was attached by covered walk to the residence of the mine superintendent.

A few feet away was a railroad track and lines of coal cars. The tunnels were a block distant and the Jenner children were warned to keep away from them and from the bunkers.

Between 80 and 90 houses stood in Old Renton on the clay company site until a flood in 1892 left the place in ruins.

Operation of the Renton mine shifted early to another portal in the gully on Benson Road at the

Black River Junction.

south city limits. An inspector's report of 1887 speaks of water seeping into the original tunnels and adds, "The Renton mine proper has not been worked for the past few years, owing to the excessive cost of pumping and the depressed market."

A short time before the water in the tunnels became a problem the Talbot mine farther south merged into the Renton mine. An old resident remembered when miners of the present century broke through into the older workings and found peculiar shovels, of a type preferred by Chinese, and wooden tracks they had built with strap iron laid on top.

The Chinese workers lived near the later Milwaukee tracks. An 1886 Harper's magazine described the row of small huts on the river bank as "steep-roofed, weather-reddened and long-shingled."

The Chinese miners had planted narrow gardens and set up tiny coops for their beloved ducks and chickens, making it "as picturesque and foreign a scene as though it were a village on the Yangtze Kiang River."

Equally picturesque was the Indian village a few miles up Cedar River.

"Father took me there," said Jenner's daughter. "We crossed Cedar River, walking on a huge fir tree with a rope attached to the bobbed-off limbs for a handhold. There was a little church in the Indian village. Mother bought berries and rag rugs from the Indian women.

"One time some Eastern Washington Indians arrived to make trouble. They were a frightening sight to us children as they passed close to our house in single file in all their regalia of war bonnets and fringed leather. After several days' powwow the horses once more passed the house in single file and the strange Indians went away as they had come."

The first standard-gauge train reached Renton in December, 1897. The Columbia and Puget Sound Railroad had bought the narrow-gauge coal line of the Seattle & Walla Walla Railroad and extended it in 1882 to Black Diamond and Franklin. Trains left Seattle on the right-of-way shared with the Northern Pacific, a third rail being laid to accommodate the narrow-gauge cars.

When it was decided to standardize the trains to Renton this meant widening the crooked three-foot tracks east from Black River Junction. At first the big engine jumped the rails so many times it could travel only four miles an hour along Black River. After a month of repairs the line was functioning properly. But Renton still seemed a long way from Seattle, as a person going to the city by train could not return until the next day.

Marshes dominated the entire southern shore of the lake. The present Shuffleton power station, had it existed then, would have been four or five blocks out in the water. When the town got a wharf in 1897 it was reached only by driving across the marsh on a plank road supported on piling. At the turn of the century there was as yet no wagon road along the shore. If one wished to drive from Seattle to Renton he went south over Beacon Hill on the old Military Road to Black River Bridge.

Renton at that time was like a Wild West town, with mud streets, two blocks of wooden sidewalks and nine saloons. Citizens carried their own lanterns at night. The village marshal put in busy weekends hauling the drunks. A shooting was not unusual.

The Changing Rivers

The landscape had changed since the early years of coal mining. Indians no longer camped at the junction of Black and Cedar Rivers. Smithers had given Indian Jim Moses an acre homesite for as long as he wished to live there. Earlier other tribesmen had camped at the junction on the Tobin place and there were Indians at times on both sides of the Cedar.

Now the tremendous cedar trees standing on the flats were gone, leaving 15-foot stumps as tokens of their passing. Slag from the mines was being used to fill the swamps. One can find it under the Boeing plant and the Renton airport.

Between 1910 and 1912 another change took place, when the course of the Cedar River was altered so that it emptied into Lake Washington. A commercial waterway district was organized to accomplish this diversion. Black River disappeared when the ship canal was built a few years later.

A long-time resident told of living west of the present airport, where her husband, Ferry Burrows, owned the Burrows Winter and Summer Pleasure Resort, which comprised a five-acre tract on the shore and a boat house with numerous canoes to rent.

Earlier her father-in-law and husband operated boats on Black River, towing logs. The younger Burrows often drove rafts, which meant riding logs, poling them along, getting them out of jams and keeping them from hanging up on brush and snags.

A boom, brought down the lake to the mouth of Black River, would be opened and long lines of logs let out, one at a time, to float downstream. About two weeks were required to maneuver the raft to its destination at a mill on the Sound. Usually six men went with it.

Mrs. Burrows, who arrived late in 1896 at what is now Bryn Mawr, said not a house then stood between Black River and Rainier Beach. Her first home was a cabin on piles. The elder Burrows built it on a little island near the bank at Black River to accommodate hunters. Duck hunting and fishing were so good here this was why the family went into the resort business.

What was left of Black River a few years ago.

Once in her first year Mrs. Burrows was alone with two small children when the water rose until it entered the house.

"I had to wear rubbers and walk on a plank to get to my bed," she recalled. "I put the wood on a chair to keep it dry for the stove."

Seattle's Southeast End

So swampy was the south end of the lake that tracks of the Renton Electric Railway in 1897 were laid on a trestle south of Rainier Beach.

Seattle streets in that area received names reminiscent of the Joseph Dunlap family. Henderson was his wife's maiden name; Pearl Street came from a name given several girls in the family and Fontanelle was their old home town in Iowa.

With Dunlaps on both sides of the lake, since son Charles had gone to Juanita, they went back and forth frequently by rowboat. Joseph towed the cedar raft he had logged on his farm across to the East Side to be sawed at Dorr Forbes' mill.

Charles, a Civil War veteran who both logged and taught at the Juanita School, was killed by a falling tree limb in 1886. His daughter, seven at the time, was sent to live at the grandfather's for a year. She remembered that he had a field planted to tobacco and let her ride the mule when he cultivated his acreage.

Part of Dunlap's land was marshy, an extension of a swamp reaching almost to Rainier Avenue and on the north separating Pritchard Island from the mainland. On older maps this was called Young's Island, for Andrew B. Young, who bought it in

Buildings at the Brighton Beach farm of Judge Everett Smith. Photo taken in the 1890s with Mercer Island in the background. The Martha Washington School later stood on the property. *Seattle Times photo courtesy of Harold V. Smith.*

1883. At the turn of the century Alfred James Pritchard was living there.

A.B. Matthiesen spent most of his life in that section after his father John (Jurgen) purchased 80 acres in 1880. The son recalled going with his brothers to the big swamp south of Atlantic City and lying on top of a beaver dam as large as a room while waiting for ducks to fly overhead so he could shoot them. The place abounded in muskrats.

In those days a skid road Dunlap had used went down to the lake at Henderson Street.

The Matthiesen house was built of lumber the father had taken in back pay owed him as head sawyer in the Meiggs mill at Port Madison. It was towed down the lake in a raft manipulated with a windlass and rowboat.

The mill wanted the elder Matthiesen back, so his wife and oldest son did the farming. The boys sold butter and eggs to the miners at Newcastle.

"Once a week," Matthiesen said, "Some of us would make a trip across the lake in a rowboat, taking all day to go and come. We started early and left the boat at May Creek, then walked up a steep trail to the top of the hill and went the rest of the way on the old coal-tramway grade. The whole walk was about three miles. We peddled house-to-house to regular customers. There was no market for vegetables and eggs in Seattle, so that was why we went so far."

Occasionally Matthiesen's father sold coal, obtaining a scowload at the Renton bunkers and taking orders for it. He made deliveries with his wagon and team. When the canal was built his coal business ended. The change in water level left his landing high and dry on the beach.

Very few neighbors lived along this part of the lakeshore. John Wilson had a farm extending as far south as Myrtle Street. North of him was Walter Graham, whose holdings reached to Juneau Street and took in Uplands Addition and the narrow neck of the Bailey Peninsula (Seward Park).

Judge Everett Smith purchased the John Wilson farm and bent his efforts toward raising a subsidy from property owners for extension of the electric railway to Rainier Beach. It started running January 1, 1891 but was not completed until March. Smith did not move his family into the house until the line was in full operation. "We had to cut a trail through the forest from Holly Street and it was a wild walk after dark," a son recalled.

The trail to Rainier Avenue was through dense timber and visitors insisted they saw bears and a cougar along the way. Judge Smith thought they might have seen his two St. Bernard dogs, which ran loose.

The judge platted Brighton Beach and named the streets. When the family moved there logging had not begun on the southern shore of Mercer Island nor on the east side of the Bailey Peninsula. In the winter when the lake was high the peninsula often became an island and the isthmus could be crossed by rowboat.

William E. Bailey bought the peninsula in 1889 from Philip Ritz for $26,000. In the same year he acquired approximately 20 acres of lakeshore near Genesee Street which John S. Maggs had proved up on and sold in 1872 to Henry Webster. This was exactly what Maggs had also done at Webster Point

Hydroplane pits at Wetmore Slough. *Photo by Greg Gilbert*

in Laurelhurst. When Mrs. Webster inherited the tract she sold it to Bailey, who in turn disposed of it in March, 1891 to the Eastern Investment Co. The latter bought much land in the boom period preceding the economic crash of 1893. The acreage reverted to the Bailey family in 1909.

Bailey was from Harrisburg, Pa., where his father had an ironworks. The Seattle fire created a need for buildings and Bailey immediately engaged in hotel construction and other realty developments. He became sole owner of The Seattle Press-Times.

Immediately north of the property Bailey purchased from the Webster estate was a logged-off tract which Guy Phinney bought in 1883 and platted as Maynard's Lake Washington Addition. Here were orchards and a boat landing.

Farther north was Frank Wetmore's place on the west side of Wetmore Slough (now Stanley Sayres Memorial Park). Frank was the son of Seymour Wetmore, a New Yorker, who had brought his family west with the Longmire wagon train in 1853. His wife was a member of the Woodin family and they all joined in founding Seattle's first tannery and shoe factory.

The Woodins and Wetmores took homesteads at Columbia City, Seymour's land being near Rainier Avenue and Charleston Street. Woodin moved from his claim to the Sammamish Valley.

Frank Wetmore purchased his own property toward the end of 1878 from Philip Ritz.

The slough extended from Charleston to Genesee Streets. Once there was talk of converting this depression into a canal, to make Columbia City a seaport. At other times it was considered for a small-boat haven and for a sunken garden.

In April, 1937 Seattle filled Lake Washington Boulevard across the mouth of the slough, putting an end to these proposals. But that was before the age of hydroplane racing, which really brought the slough into the headlines.

Canal Proposed Through Beacon Hill

Polk's Seattle city map of 1902 draws attention to a vanished dream, where it indicates south of Hanford Street the eastern end of "the proposed Seattle & Lake Washington Company's canal," which would have cut through Beacon Hill, the shortest distance between the lake and salt water.

Seattle had been talking of a canal for 40 years and had petitioned Congress to empower King County to excavate one and to keep all of the land reclaimed by lowering the water. In years past six different routes had been proposed: by the Duwamish and Black River, by way of Pike or Battery Street to Lake Union, from Lake Union along Mercer Street to Elliott Bay, from Smith Cove to Salmon Bay and Lake Union, through Beacon Hill to Lake Washington and from Shilshole Bay to Lake Union.

By the 1890's the canal to Puget Sound had become a main political issue, one of the objectives in the battle between Tacoma and Seattle for commercial supremacy. In February, 1889 a Navy commission of five members was escorted around the lake in the steamship *Kirkland.* Two years later the Board of Engineers reported on the proposal of a canal through Lake Union to Shilshole Bay with a 400-foot lock. However, the costlier route across to Smith Cove received approval of the Secretary of War.

President Harrison was drawn into the controversy when he visited in May, 1891 and was given the grand tour in the *Kirkland.*

Although all canal proposals suffered from Democratic opposition in 1892, the waterway was strongly urged again the following year after hard times had struck. Canal construction was visualized as a means of alleviating unemployment.

In April, 1894 an open meeting was held to discuss what should be done. One statement was made that until the little canal had been cut between the lakes and a small wooden dam had been placed at the outlet of Lake Union at Fremont by the Washington Improvement Co. (composed of Denny, Smithers, Kinnear and others) no losses to farmers had occurred. The work in the 1880's, however, had caused bars to form at the mouths of the Cedar and Black Rivers, which in turn forced them to flow across into White River and submerge a vast area of tillable lands.

Another thing had happened. Black River formerly had afforded a good outlet for logs; now this was no longer true.

The meeting was much wrought up about current developments. The Washington Improvement Co. had proposed to sell its franchise and its property and to consider a proposition of the Northwest Bridge Co. to enlarge the existing canal.

Farmers at the meeting thought that more meddling might make conditions worse. Their prime consideration was that all of the water of Cedar River must be made to flow into the lake. Then there would be no trouble, as White River was lower than Lake Washington and could not overflow into it.

These people were convinced that the floods were due as much to artificial causes as to the elements.

"We are not here to build a canal for ships," one man declared. "That is a hackneyed subject. What we want is relief from the unnatural overflow on our farms, caused by the tampering with the natural outlets of the lakes in years past."

The farmers' movement was much in earnest and it was believed that if consent could be secured in the proper quarters the canal outlet would be enlarged, even if it were necessary to go through University property to do so. An expert who had investigated various schemes said it was possible to put in a canal 10 feet deep at the Lake Washington level and 27 feet wide and carry off four feet depth of the lake in three to four months. He was for using the existing outlet, widening and improving it, not digging a new one.

Matters did not progress beyond discussion until the following June 22 when the Seattle and Lake Washington Waterways Co. was incorporated, with a totally different agenda. It was prepared to excavate a canal, not at Union Bay, but through Beacon Hill. Former Governor Eugene Semple was the moving spirit in this scheme and the Mississippi Valley Trust Co. of St. Louis was its most powerful backer. Public subscriptions in Seattle netted more than $50,000 in guaranteed subsidy.

Semple's scheme was to dig a canal a mile long and 300 feet wide through the tide flats at the mouth of the Duwamish River. The flats were to be filled with earth from the excavation. The canal would be dug eastward from the head of the East Waterway and lead into a passage two miles long through Beacon Hill at Hanford Street.

Work began in July, 1895, the dredge *Python* opening the East Waterway, where bulkheads were built.

Long delays were caused by litigation as to ownership of the tidelands. Earth brought up by dredging was spread over 175 acres of flats before funds were exhausted. The sluicing of Beacon Hill ran into trouble because of slippery blue clay (the old glacial deposits). The whole operation became so involved in legal battles and shortages of funds that work ceased in 1897. The old canal strip was declared vacated in 1914.

"Difficulties amounting to irreducible obstacles barred its construction," said the final report on the Hanford Street canal.

The planned cut through the hill was to have been 80 feet wide at the bottom and a maximum of 340 feet. It was to cost more than $70,000,000.

So much for that canal scheme, but the issue was by no means dead.

Landslide!

Landslides were not unusual in the long history of Lake Washington, as borne out by the existence of sunken forests, but the only bad one in historic times occurred between Dearborn and Norman Streets in Seattle in 1898.

Midway between these two streets, at the foot of Charles, was the sawmill founded by Guy Phinney. He was a Nova Scotian, a cousin of Arthur Phinney, who was prominent in logging at Port Ludlow.

The cousin's success may have inspired Guy. In 1883 he acquired the property on the lakeshore and two years later the city directory showed him as president of the Lake Washington Mill Co. The sawmill may have been the first industrial plant on the lake, depending on whether Phinney or Dorr Forbes at Juanita got a head start. Phinney soon transferred his attention to other developments and by 1889 the mill had changed hands twice and John Sanford Taylor was the current owner. His name is the one most often associated with it.

Taylor, a native of Scotland, had a mill in Minnesota when he made a trip west and decided to lease the Phinney establishment. He sold out his eastern holdings and took over the plant on the lake, keeping it running day and night while he rushed erection of a new building.

A newspaper account of 1895 states, "He was compelled to enlarge his facilities and erected a planing mill on the bluff overlooking the sawmill, connecting the two with an inclined tramway."

The article described the establishment as one of the most up-to-date in the Puget Sound country and

Perhaps the earliest sawmill on Lake Washington. This shows how the reeds grew everywhere along the shallow parts of the shoreline. *Courtesy Seattle Historical Society.*

Old Taylor Mill Towboat - from *Carl Weber Collection*

said, "Both mills are equipped with the latest improved machinery of the best makes, such as steam feed, live rolls and endless log haul-up, their capacity being 75,000 feet per day."

Taylor had his own logging camp and logging railway on Lake Sammamish.

The tramline of the mill ran up Charles Street to "Taylor's Upper Town Mill" at 30th Avenue S. and Judkins Street. This tramline vanished one day in 1898 when some 75 acres of the steep slope suddenly moved down into the lake, jarring 16 houses off their foundations and pushing the lower mill out of business.

Seattleites came to gape at the sight, looking down from the hilltop on houses pitched helter skelter. It had been a season of unparalleled floods over the western part of the state and some minor slides had occurred near the lake, but this was the worst of all. Some of the earth which went down piled up in the lake and modern shore homes stand now on the hump it made.

No landslide deterred Taylor from his chosen calling and a few years later he erected a new mill by a small stream midway between Rainier Beach and Bryn Mawr. He built out over the lake on pilings. A community grew up on shore near the mill, known officially as the Rainier Beach Lumber Co.

The Charles Street location meanwhile became the property of the Sutherland Mill Ltd., which rehabilitated the plants and they remained in operation until the one on shore burned May 10, 1911 in an incendiary fire.

Wanted: Pure Water

Pollution of Lake Washington was a live subject the year of the great Seattle fire, 1889, when the municipality purchased the Spring Hill Water Co., the largest of six systems which supplied the city.

A pumping plant had been installed on the lakeshore at the foot of Holgate Street in 1884 after the company's springs on the west side of First Hill proved inadequate. The new pumps delivered from 1,500,000 to 2,000,000 gallons daily to a reservoir newly constructed at 13th Avenue S. and Holgate Street, site of the present Beacon Hill Playground. This pipeline from the lake supplied the city's water until 1901, when the Cedar River system was inaugurated.

The fire 12 years earlier demonstrated the inadequacy of the Spring Hill Water Company's equipment and the voters had to decide whether to continue depending on a private corporation or operate their own facilities. The municipality paid $350,000 for the Spring Hill properties and set about expanding them as a temporary expedient until another source could be explored. Use of Cedar River already was being considered.

A report by Prof. James Parkinson that year pointed out that organic matter in the lake was increasing and the natural drainage of a large area flowed toward it. He said that unless expensive pumping plants were constructed to carry sewage into Elliott Bay, this material, coupled with the waste from commercial development, "surely would add year by year to contamination despite the utmost care exercised to prevent it."

Nevertheless, Seattle enlarged the Holgate Street pumping plant in 1890. The largest of its four pumps delivered 7,000,000 gallons daily.

A trestle carried the steel pipe far enough out over the water so that the lake could be tapped at a depth of 30 or 40 feet below the surface. Power for the pumping station was generated with bargeloads of coal brought from the Newcastle bunkers.

Mayor Robert Moran in 1890 declared that with the new improvements the work would last for generations. He reckoned without the bacteria that were multiplying in the lake.

In August, 1907 Seattle experienced its greatest typhoid epidemic. By September the number of cases had reached a grand total of 570. The city health officer insisted, "The city's water supply has nothing to do with the typhoid fever cases prevalent." He thought the infection had been brought from logging and vacation camps outside the city.

More than half a century later a researcher put the blame where it belonged—on Lake Washington.

Lack of rain that summer had lowered water in the reservoirs and the city fathers, afraid of fire, filled the one on Beacon Hill with 10,000 gallons pumped from the lake. As soon as the rains set in, the reservoir, leased from a contracting firm, was returned to its owners, but the damage already had been done. Persons living near Jackson Street received the contaminated water in their pipes and typhoid broke out immediately after the incubation period expired.

In 1909 during the Alaska Yukon Pacific Exposition water was again pumped from the lake to the present University grounds and in a suspiciously brief time 21 persons living and working there contracted typhoid. Two hundred visitors also were down with it.

After these experiences the city shied away from running lake water into pipes. When the Cedar River line broke down citizens were cautioned to boil all drinking water and, although the lake was once more resorted to, no epidemic resulted.

As late as the Second World War illness occurred at the shipyard in Houghton because employees drank polluted lake water.

For many years scattered dwellers on the East Side and on Mercer Island thrust pipes hundreds of feet into the lake and continued to use it as a fresh water source. Eventually the end had to come; there were just too many people living roundabout.

The Cable Car Line

Another improvement about the time of the pumping station was construction of the Lake Washington Cable Railroad.

Leschi had been attracting so many visitors during the summer months that the stages running out to the beach at this place were unable to accommodate the traffic. A promoter from San Francisco, Fred E. Sander, persuaded a number of business men that a cable way was the answer, if they could raise a subsidy for it. A franchise was granted in 1884, but four years elapsed before the line was completed.

The cars ran out Yesler Way through an unbroken wilderness and crossed a gorge on a trestle 500 feet long and 200 feet above ground at the highest point. The route returned by way of Jackson Street over another trestle 140 feet high. The round trip was more than five miles, parts of the line being so unsafe that "extreme care and ingenuity" were required to operate cars over it.

Formal opening of the cable route was on September 28, 1888. Elegant lithographed cards, bearing a view of Lake Washington with Mount Rainier in the distance, had been issued to public officials, the press and other invited guests. Cars departed from in front of Seattle's Occidental Hotel.

Visitors were taken to view the 120-horsepower Corliss steam engine which ran the cable drums. At noon the roundhouse doors were thrown open and a gala feast was served, champagne and claret flowing and cigars being liberally distributed.

Former Mayor John Leary, one of the speakers, related that the company had spent $200,000 on the line and planned to invest another $50,000 in a pavilion at Leschi, rolling stock and an excursion steamboat.

Real estate sales multiplied, 1,569 houses were built along the new line that summer, a pavilion was erected on the lakeshore with a seating capacity for 4,000 persons and cars made connections with the steamships *Kirkland* and *C.C. Calkins*, running to Mercer Island and the East Side.

Nevertheless the cable line was in shaky condition not only as to trestle construction, but in its finan-

Cable railroad descending to Leschi Park power house.

cial structure. Then, on August 17, 1890, a car was going down the last section of the Yesler line when a sudden gust of wind struck it, the trestle swayed and the passengers were so frightened they jumped off and clung to the railing. The gripman stayed with the car, which careened wildly down. Workmen saw it coming and threw ties on the track to stop it at the bottom.

After this happening some replacements had to be made. The company went through a receivership and two reorganizations that year. The entire system was rebuilt, the cable was electric powered and in June, 1900 the Jackson Street portion was discontinued, the cars running back and forth only on Yesler Way.

An old advertising booklet shows the little Yesler cars departing from the city every four minutes and, in afternoons and evenings, every three minutes. Not bad service until one remembers how few passengers they hauled in a single trip; the average car had seats for only 22 persons.

It was the first cable car line north of San Francisco.

Leschi Park

Leschi was Seattle's first ambitious park. It had a zoo of sorts, a bandstand and gardens and the big pavilion for special events. Until the cable line was constructed boat passenger service on the lake had been irregular, but now it picked up.

Mrs. Alla Olds Luckenbill, daughter of the Mercer Island settler, remembered that early in 1885 the only resident at Leschi was a solitary man raising hogs, ducks and chickens. The sandy beach was littered with driftwood and Indians still camped there.

By 1890 the settlement had increased and included the ferry landing, a hotel, store and a boathouse. More boats were around and by 1902 among them were several of that new species, the powerboat. A man who cleared timber north of Leschi owned the *Mable S.*, the third gas boat on the lake. The only way it could take on fuel was to run to the wharf at the end of Madison Street and pick up barrels of naphtha delivered there.

The park tract, bought in 1895, was speedily improved. Among its attractions were a South American puma, monkeys and sea lions, which were fed daily at 4 p.m. for the entertainment of visitors.

Once a tightrope performer was featured, his rope being rigged from the powerhouse to the pavilion. Another time a balloon ascension was staged. The bag was filled by building a fire in a pit at the end of a tunnel, which conducted the hot air into the balloon. A woman went up and came down in a parachute; a man went up and splashed into the lake when he landed. Once monkeys were sent up.

Leschi was a gathering place of small boats, as it still is. From early in the century a tale of circumnavigation has been handed down that could not be duplicated now.

Charles R. Adams told the story. He explained that when Laurelhurst was being promoted in 1906 Frank Atwood, a real estate man, offered the purchaser of each tract there or at Sand Point a new 16-foot boat with inboard motor, so as to save the buyer the great part of a day driving by team to his property.

Atwood ordered 20 boats, delivered at Seattle. He engaged Adams' father to see if he could bring them to the lake. Father and son left the Atwood dock at Leschi, went down Black River into the

Pavilion - at Leschi Park, *Seattle Historical Society*

The power house at Leschi Park. Photo by Frank La Roche circa 1890. *University of Washington Library.*

Leschi Park boat landing beside the power house.

Duwamish and picked up three of the new boats near the present ferry terminal. They took them in tow and steered for Shilshole Bay.

By then boats could go as far as Fremont without much difficulty because in 1884 the Lake Washington Improvement Co. had employed Chinese to dig a passage three quarters of a mile long where a stream from Lake Union trickled toward Salmon Bay. At the head of this passage was a small wooden lock with gates and a fishway for spawning salmon to enter. At its south end was a spillway about six feet wide and no gate. Over this Adams portaged the boats one at a time into Lake Union, mooring the rest to the bank while he shoved each craft over the obstruction.

When all were in the lake he hooked them up and proceeded to Portage Bay. Then came the most difficult passage. Water from Lake Washington ran through the narrow ditch, completed a year or more after the Fremont passage.

Adams explained, "Dad got into the water knee deep and pushed each boat along while I pulled from the bank. Sometimes they stuck on the Union Bay side, which was very shallow, but we pushed them off and finally got them hooked up and in tow to Leschi. Dad had proved you could bring boats through, but Frank Atwood decided there was an easier way. He hired a teamster to bring the others on a dray."

Boats at Leschi Park landing. *University of Washington Library*

Dock and warehouse at Leschi. *University of Washington Library*

This early boat is not identified. So many sailboats indicate the photo was apparently made on a holiday, probably off Madrona or Leschi. Picture by Frank LaRoche circa 1890. *University of Washington Library.*

Camping near Madrona.

Madrona and Madison Park

As late as the 1890's few houses were between Leschi and the end of Madison Street and no roads joined the two places. The Puget Mill Co. owned some of the land between. In summer one could find families camping in tents at Madrona, going there by boat from Leschi.

Adams said Indians frequented Madrona Park until about 1906. From them he heard a curious bit of folklore about the lake. They told him that once upon a time there was a small island in the center between Madison Park and Kirkland and that about 30 Indians lived there. One night the island disappeared from sight and took all of them with it.

Another association Adams had with Madrona was catching baby eels in springs and streams running into the lake. He earned spending money by catching them for a pharmacist at Twenty-third and Yesler Way who paid 15 cents apiece for them but never told the use to which they were put.

When bicycling was in fashion in the 1890's a favorite route was a cinder path between Leschi and Madison Parks and north into the present Arboretum. This course was the genesis of Lake Washington Boulevard, later laid out along the same route and extended to Seward Park. Eventually the highway circled the lake, although

on the East Side it was not always close to the water.*

At the turn of the century Madison Park had a large pavilion where concerts were given by groups such as the 40-piece Wagner's Band. Taking one's girl friend in a canoe out on the water to listen to the music was the smart thing for the younger set. Or else one could listen and decorously imbibe beer in the vicinity of the pavilion.

The Pioneer Society of the State of Washington in 1902 was given a lot on the lakeshore for a place in which to hold its reunions. It had a wooden building where members gathered for dinner in relays, then adjourned to the park for a program. Another gift of cash in 1909 enabled the organization to erect a brick building on the lot, now the oldest structure in that vicinity.

Note: Roads near the lake began in the south end in 1878 with a route from Renton to Coal Creek, then inland to the mines. Next year an extension of the Telegraph or Military Road was surveyed along the northwest bank and up the Sammamish River to Bothell. Hard surfacing did not begin until 1908 when Seattle and Lake Forest Park were connected. After that, in 1912, four miles of brick paving, laid by hand, were completed to Bothell. In 1917 a wooden bridge was constructed at Kenmore and the Juanita Drive Section of Lake Washington Boulevard had its beginning. In another two years there was a continuous road from Renton to Bellevue, but 13 miles were still to be paved. Work was begun surfacing the route as far as Kirkland. Gradually more sections were completed and by October, 1922 local inhabitants rejoiced that the boulevard was a reality.

Pavilion in Madison Park

The bicycle path.

Beginning of Boat Service

Before the era of automobiles and highways, if one wished to go anywhere across Lake Washington it had to be by boat. A trip to market, to the dentist or doctor or the court house had to be made in earliest times by canoe or rowboat. Later there were the wood-fired steam tugs and after that the first naphtha-driven motors, the forerunners of gasoline-powered craft.

Transportation can be said to have begun with scows used by coal miners and farmers to carry their products down the lake to Black River and into the Duwamish, thence to the Seattle waterfront. One of the Wold brothers of Issaquah is credited with having built the initial scow in the late 1860s to carry his farm produce, though Casto also appears to have had such a craft.

As early as 1869 the Territorial Legislative Council authorized operation of a ferry on the lake, but nothing came of it. The first powered vessels were the *James Mortie*, *Chehalis* and *Addie*, and there may have been another, the *Phantom*.

Some hints as to the state of travel to and from the Sammamish are gleaned from old accounts. Robert Moran told of obtaining a job at Brackett's logging camp at Bothell. The only way he could get there was to depart on the *James Mortie* from Yesler Way and go to the mouth of the Sammamish, where he transferred to the logger's boat and continued upstream to camp. Not proving a success at his new post, Moran was sent back out in the company boat and dumped at the present University of Washington campus. From there he picked his way through virgin timber and windfalls back to Seattle.

A diary kept by Mrs. Clara Colman at May Creek in 1886-7 spoke of a member of the family boarding a scow carrying cattle to Frank Wetmore's farm on the Seattle side. Another day Mrs. Colman mentioned returning from the city in a craft hired at H.G. Martin's boathouse south of Jackson Street. The same boathouse engaged to carry a court bailiff around the lake serving subpoenas.

Beginning in 1884 Laurel Shade at the head of Madison Street became the regular port of call of the steamer *Squak*, which went on the Sammamish River run and drew only eight inches of water. An engine was installed on each side and the center was covered with a cabin.

The *Squak* made stops at Wayne, two miles east of Kenmore, and next at Bothell and Woodinville. Redmond, or McRedmond's Bridge, was the last stop before Lake Sammamish. The span was located where the road from the Curtis farm near Houghton emerged from the woods, crossed the river and went on up the valley to Cottage Lake and Bear Creek.

A ditch had been dug on the section line and carried through the swamp to Squak Slough (Sammamish River) for drainage. The work had been done by the railroad contractor. The ditch had the effect of building up a dam almost to the surface. In order for the *Squak* to get over the obstruction, passengers and some of the freight had to be moved to the stern of the boat. Then a run was made and the vessel surmounted the shoal, scraping mud.

It was an adventure to go up the Sammamish at any time. The late Miss Margaret Yarno told of a trip she made to act as bridesmaid at a wedding on February 3, 1887 at Issaquah. When she boarded the *Squak* at Laurel Shade the vessel was loaded with 25 men, mostly loggers bound for Fall City and North Bend. These were packed aboard a boat with a cabin so narrow one's outstretched arms would touch both sides.

"We left at 8 a.m.," Miss Yarno said, "and arrived at Bothell at 2 p.m. I'd had no breakfast and nothing else to eat. Mrs. David C. Bothell wasn't expecting to have to feed so many passengers."

The boat whistle was tooting impatiently long before Miss Yarno finished her meal.

"Never mind, dearie, they won't go until you're through," Mrs. Bothell told her.

The boat reached the head of Lake Sammamish at 10 p.m. Next day guests journeyed from far and near in logging sleds to attend the ceremony, performed by a justice of the peace.

Miss Yarno had to get back to Seattle at once, as she was attending high school. The bride's mother was going to the city for jury duty, so her husband took the two women by rowboat as far as the bridge at Redmond. The weather was cold and they carried hot bricks to warm their feet.

"We were to take the stage from there to Houghton and board the launch *Bee*," Miss Yarno explained. "So my friend's husband turned around and went home.

"The stage never came and we walked four miles to Houghton in the snow through the dense timber. We didn't meet a soul the entire way.

"When we reached Houghton the little *Bee* had gone. Captain J.C. O'Connor owned a house there that was like a hotel. We stayed in it overnight and caught the *Bee* next morning. She made two trips daily. There was no stage when we got into Laurel Shade, so I walked the rest of the way home to Lake Union."

"Two other early boats were the *Jennie June* and the *Evril*. Neither was more than about 30 feet long. Captain James Allen, their operator, evident-

The ferry King County of Kent.

ly brought them up through the Duwamish. He did some towing on Black River. If the water was low at the south end of the lake sometimes W.P. Smith at Renton would take his team of oxen and tow the *Evril* over the bar.

Allen operated the boats from 1884 until he became postmaster at Juanita in 1889. After that he did logging and was justice of the peace.

A member of the family told how Allen found a bride. Allen Day had a homestead near present Vasa Park on Lake Sammamish and cut wood for the *Evril.* James Allen became acquainted with Day's daughter, Effie, and proposed marriage, but her father did not approve. Effie got around that by waiting elsewhere on the bank. Allen picked her up with the steamboat and they eloped.

Allen's biggest rush of business was transporting materials for construction of the Seattle, Lake Shore & Eastern Railroad. He ran regularly at that time between the end of Madison Street and Issaquah. Although the Sammamish River was a terror to navigate, sometimes on the same trip Allen would be carrying passengers and towing a bargeload of dynamite. He serviced his own boat, diving when necessary to patch the bottom. One time when he reached a bend the bow ran on one bank and the stern on the other. A team of horses pulled him off.

Allen's passengers ate beyond Woodinville and when he rounded a bend before reaching it, he would blow his whistle to indicate the number of persons he was carrying. That way Mrs. Peterson, opposite present Hollywood, knew how many persons she would be required to feed.

Steamboat buffs speak of many other boats which made lake history. The *Laura Maud* was built by J.C. O'Connor in 1887 and the *Kirkland* in 1888. For a time the *Edith E.* made daily trips for coal for the waterworks. The *Augusta* also towed coal barges and the *Reef* did log towing.

Olds on Mercer Island had the smallest steamboat, the *Alvico*, about 1888, but it was condemned because the boiler was too large and dangerous.

The *Enigma*, launched at Leschi in 1893, was so named because Captain Riddell, its owner, wondered what to call her.

The ferry *King County*, was built in 1899 to run between Madison Street and Kirkland. She sank in 1907.

County wharves were acquired in 1900 at either end of the ferry run, followed by the Furth dock in

1902, Mercer Slough and Juanita in 1905, Newport, Medina and Kennydale in 1907.

Polk's 1902 Seattle map shows a boat line from Madison Street to Houghton, Kirkland and Juanita. Madrona had a ferry landing and Leschi had two ferry lines, one to Mercer Island and the other calling at Meydenbauer Bay, Mercer Slough and Newcastle Landing.

In the age of competitive boat lines the *C.C. Calkins*, *Winnifred*, *Acme* and *Lady of the Lake* all were built on Lake Washington. The *W.C. Harrington* was built on the Sound and brought around and put on the Sammamish River run.

Anderson and His Steamboats

The real shipping magnate was John L. Anderson, who by 1911 owned the *Fortuna*, *Urania*, *Atlanta*, *Triton*, *Aquilo*, *Xanthus*, *Cyrene*, *Dorothy*, and *L.T. Haas.* They were then serving Leschi and Madison Street, running to East Seattle, Medina, Kirkland, Bellevue, Factoria, Kennydale, Beaux Arts, Houghton, Cozy Cove, Wilburton, Wildwood Park, Atlanta Park and Fortuna Park.

An advertising folder dating from the second decade of the present century showed the excursion boat *Fortuna* at such places as the Anderson shipyard in Houghton where Atlanta Park was also located. Its main feature was a dance pavilion which later became the mold loft and pipe shop. Another stop was Fortuna Park on Mercer Island, a 10-acre tract with pavilion, kitchen and dressing rooms. The folder indicated Newport was important because automobile parties bound for Snoqualmie Pass debarked there. Kennydale was cited as the place where milk was "exported by the ton."

The *Fortuna's* excursion required three hours and the brochure promised patrons: "In all the world there's no trip like this."

Anderson's original shipyard was at Leschi. His beginnings were modest. He was a Swedish immigrant who landed in Seattle in 1888 and obtained odd jobs around the city, one as deckboy on the *George M. Elder.* When the *C.C. Calkins* went on the Mercer Island run in 1890 he joined her as deckhand, then rose to fireman, purser and mate. Before he was 22 he qualified as a pilot and soon was the master of the *Calkins.*

He had loaned some of his savings to the owners of the *Winnifred* and the only way of collecting his money was by taking a half interest in the craft. Then he bought the other half. After that he

Ferry connections were important to lakeshore boosters.
University of Washington Library

Steamer Triton at Fortuna Park on Mercer Island. This is a typical holiday crowd. *University of Washington Library.*

purchased the steamer *Quickstep*, removed her machinery and put it into the *Lady of the Lake* and sold this vessel at a profit for service on the Sound. Next he built the *Leschi* for the Madison Park run, or rather he assembled her after the parts were brought overland from the West Waterway. She was too big to bring in by any other route.

Then he built the *Acme*, sold her and bought the *Cyrene* and *Xanthus*, the launch *Ramona* and sternwheeler *Mercer*. The Alaska Yukon Pacific Exposition was soon to open and he believed there would be big business in lake excursions, so he set out to corner the trade. But first he looked for a better shipyard site.

Houghton seemed the logical place, for it had drawn boatbuilders ever since Captain O'Connor built the *Squak*, the Curtis brothers constructed the *Elfin* and Easter, the *Edith E*. By 1901 a yard on the beach had been opened by the Bartsch and Tompkins Transportation Co., with their meager equipment. The completed craft sometimes were floated out of the lake through Black River at times of high water.

Anderson purchased the yard in 1907, improved it and sought orders. He built a lighthouse tender and a couple of ferries, the *Issaquah* and the *Lincoln*. At first the yard employed 25 to 30 men. A photograph from 1908 indicates how modestly Anderson began his establishment. The view shows two little boats on the beach and the derelict *Gazelle* out in the water, its boiler supplying steam for the yard. One long low shed was the sawmill that cut the lumber. Hoisting was done by a marine engine.

Two of the products at Houghton were the 78-foot sister ships *Triton* and *Aquilo*, launched by

Anderson for his own steamboat company to add to its fleet in 1909, the year of the fair. Anderson had 14 vessels ready to handle the crowds. That was the golden year of steamboating on Lake Washington. Besides the Anderson fleet there were six other craft operated by competitors. One of them was the King County ferry *Washington* running between Madison Park and Kirkland.

Anderson provided 15 minute service between Leschi, Madrona, Madison Park and the fair grounds. Five daily two hour excursions also left the fair grounds and five more operated from Leschi around Mercer Island. Visitors could have a 25 mile ride for 25 cents. It was estimated that 1,500,000 persons that summer sampled at least one Lake Washington excursion.

Meanwhile regular runs were maintained to East Seattle, the west and north sides of Mercer Island, Newcastle Landing, Medina, Bellevue, Kirkland, Juanita, Houghton and Fairweather Bay. Interlaken Steamship Co. competed with Anderson between Leschi and Bellevue, but after the fair was over he absorbed the company and took over its two boats, the *Wildwood* and *L. T. Haas*.

For 30 years Anderson was an important figure on the lake. His shipyard expanded gradually until it reached out for contracts during the First World War and became the Anderson Shipbuilding Corp. Its first wartime order was for four 3,500-ton freighters for the French government. In 1918 the yard was crowded with lumber piles. Other lumber was stored on rafts and snaked ashore by steam donkey when needed. The place rang with activity. Air hammers made it the noisiest spot on the East Side.

New Owners for the Shipyard

Anderson sold out in 1923 to the Lake Washington Shipyard Co., of which Charles A. Burckhardt was president. He was one of the

The Lake Washington shipyard at Houghton taken probably about 1947 when wartime buildings were still there. *Seattle Times photo from Kirkland Historical Society.*

Steamship L.T. Haas. *University of Washington Library*

principal Alaska salmon packers and in the next few years the company turned out a large number of vessels for the salmon industry in the north and repaired hundreds of small craft. In 1925 the firm began building steel as well as wooden vessels, conversion of the Great Lakes steamer *Chippewa* into a Puget Sound ferry being its first move in this direction. In 1933 it handled its most unusual order, rebuilding a burned-out San Francisco ferry to create the stream-lined *Kalakala*.

In 1940 the yard took its first government contracts and between Pearl Harbor and February, 1945 it had repaired 477 ships. It constructed 25 seaplane tenders, four motor torpedo tenders, four net tenders and two survey ships. Its roll of employees jumped to near 6,000, of whom 175 were wartime guards and watchmen. Housing had to be built to accommodate the workers and the ferry *Leschi* made special trips from Seattle carrying others.

The yard had a distinguished record, but when the war was over it was put up for sale. Skinner Corp. was the purchaser. Some of the facilities went to the Alaska Terminal and Stevedoring Co. for winter tie-up of vessels from the North. Other parts were disposed of for various uses. For several years the corporation considered apartment house developments but finally it converted the entire property into training quarters for the Seahawks professional football team. Demolition crews have left little trace of the marine activity that once centered there.

The University of Washington Stadium dominates the shoreline near the campus. *Photo by Greg Gilbert.*

The University Moves

By 1890 the University of Washington had outgrown its 10-acre tract in what is now the center of the city and needed to spread out. Edmond S. Meany, active as a faculty member and administrator, was also a member of the State Legislature. He busied himself with seeking a new site to conform with provisions in certain quitclaim deeds which required it must be within six miles of the old one. A section of school land appeared most desirable in order to eliminate private profit or speculation.

Meany found that three tracts qualified for the purpose—the present Fort Lawton, Jefferson Park and Interlachen (now the campus). He favored the last, but realized he had the best chance of getting it if he made the choice appear to come from the 1891 legislature. He arranged to bring members of the joint committee to Seattle for personal inspection of the sites. They traveled on railroad passes, readily available in those days. A small boat was chartered at the south end of Lake Union to carry them to Interlachen, then covered with heavy timber.

The land was a fractional section bordering the two lakes for one and a half miles. The forest covered more than 200 acres. Members of the committee were so pleased with the site they boosted Meany on a high stump and urged him to make a speech. It was apparent at once that they approved his selection.

While the committee had been hypnotized, legislative leaders were not so easily carried away by the project. They limited the purchase to 160 acres out of the 580 in the fractional section. Meany was disappointed by his partial victory and feared that the remainder would be divided and the lakeshore would be grabbed up. When the next legislative session opened in 1893 he was ready with arguments for a larger campus.

"Cornell," he declared, "has its beautiful Lake Cayuga. Wisconsin has Lake Mendota, but two beautiful freshwater lakes are none too many to lave the shores of the university campus which bears the name of the Father of Our Country."

His eloquence won the day and the award was for 341.76 acres of upland and nearly 250 acres of lowland and water within pierhead lines.

Among the legislators were many influential timbermen and Meany, to win their support, pointed out the advantages of forestry study and the

Cascades on the grounds of the Alaska Yukon Pacific Exposition in 1909. The United States government building is in the background. *Seattle Times photo from Mrs. W.G. Visser collection.*

maintenance of an arboretum as a laboratory for guiding future generations in perpetuating timber resources.

Meany regarded this as a serious obligation and in 1895 a landscape architect who had been employed was given the title of "curator of the arboretum." Together the two men selected the best specimens of native trees to be saved from the virgin forest on the campus. They collected and planted many from foreign lands. Meany's vision was that the entire tract would serve as the arboretum. This accounts for the interesting trees still to be seen scattered about the grounds, where they have missed the inroads of shovels and bulldozers.

In those first years on the new location the University annually observed Campus Day, when students joined in opening paths, cutting away logs and bridging wet places. Blasting of stumps was handled by professors and students of mining engineering.

Portions of the tract were still in a wild state when in 1906 Seattleites conceived the plan for the Alaska Yukon Pacific Exposition. That June a citizens committee requested the board of regents to permit use of 250 acres of the campus for the fair, which was readily granted, as certain benefits in the way of improvements and permanent buildings were visualized.

The exhibit buildings were erected on the southern part of the campus, with the present "Frosh Pond" as the center of the main plaza. The principal entrance was on N.E. 40th Street, with another on the Montlake end. A park extended along the Lake Washington side and amusements were on a street going up from Lake Union and paralleling 15th Avenue N.E. Structures were all

painted old ivory and the general effect was pleasing, in view of the magnificent setting of lakes, mountains and timber.

The exposition ran from June 1 through October 16, 1909 and took in 2,765,683 paid admissions. It was a financial success and the university gained between 20 and 25 structures of varying degrees of durability. Several are still in use.

The grounds of the lower campus were improved and planted with gardens too elaborate for the struggling school to maintain. However, the grading and construction had destroyed much of Meany's arboretum and the campus was no longer referred to officially as such.

The idea of an arboretum did not die completely, but it was 1924 before there was definite hope of reviving it. Adequate space within the campus was gone, but nearby in Montlake was a park which offered possibilities.

Some of the last timber logged within the city limits of Seattle was taken off a tract owned by Rolland Denny, which afterward became Washington Park. A small stream flowed through it into the Union Bay swamp.

The city park commissioners offered the tract for an arboretum, but its development was delayed by the economic depression and limited funds. Finally in 1934 the project was in a position to qualify legally for federal funds and got on its feet. The 267-acre tract is leased from Seattle and has been made into a place of great beauty, with a Japanese garden as one of the outstanding attractions.

This feature was completed in 1960. It included a tea house (since destroyed by an arson fire), the gift of the City of Tokyo and two stone lanterns, gifts of the City of Kobe. The garden, covering four acres, was laid out by one of Japan's foremost landscape designers. In it are 3,000 shrubs, more than 400

Japanese Garden - at the Arboretum *Greg Gilbert photo*

Fallen leaves herald the coming of autumn in the Arboretum. *Photo by Greg Gilbert.*

The old shell house on the University of Washington campus. *Photo by Greg Gilbert*

trees, 11 hand-carved lanterns, and twin artificial mountains created out of rocks hauled from the Snoqualmie River.

Another development tied to the presence of the University is the crew racing. Early any spring morning one may see shells on the lake and hear the voice of a coach with his megaphone.

Support for this activity was first sought about 1899. Among the donations offered was a promise from the Puget Mill Co. of some timber near Lake Washington, providing the University would find a way to cut it. Fifty students turned out for a logging bee on the present Broadmoor Golf Course.

At that time the entire district from the top of Capitol Hill to the lake was thick forest, in which were some especially large cedar trees.

The logs cut by the students were used to build a crew house and float not far from the present headquarters. At first the races were between classes and no coaches were employed. In 1903 the initial intercollegiate race was held on the lake, using four-oared shells and no coxswains.

In 1906 Hiram Conibear, who had been a trainer with the Chicago White Sox baseball team, arrived in Seattle and put rowing on the map. He raised money to keep the sport going. His interest was roused after he watched the amateur crews work out on the lake and saw that most of what they did was wrong. Next year the first eight-oared shell races were held. Since then the University of Washington has maintained a strong interest in its crew and has carried off its share of trophies.

While speaking of the shell house mention should be made of the canoes that can be rented there by anyone for paddling amid what is left of Union Bay marsh. This place has undergone great changes since the level of the lake was altered. The north side of the present ship canal was formerly the big marsh, but it has been largely obliterated by an extensive sanitary fill. The south side of the canal, formerly under water, is now the main scene of swamp life. Here one can find almost every type of bird that visits Lake Washington, as well as beaver, muskrat and other mammals. The city gradually

Canoeing in its heyday.

has encroached upon the marsh and it is not what it was in 1951 when two naturalists, Harry W. Higman and Earl J. Larrison, wrote an entire book about the wildlife there.

Today a nature walk starts near the Museum of History and Industry in Montlake, the elevated path extending far out among the reeds. Bird lovers like to visit tiny Foster Island (named for a trapper who made it his headquarters in pioneer times). Although traffic over the Evergreen Point Bridge whizzes by, this island is still a bird refuge.

The Canal a Reality

Most of the foregoing has dealt with the lake that was larger than we know it today. The time of change arrived in 1911.

To fill in the story, one must go back a few years to the effort of former Governor Semple to cut through Beacon Hill. Regardless of his project, the Navy had investigated a proposal to create a fresh-water basin for vessels in Lake Union. A board of engineer officers had recommended the route from Shilshole Bay to the lake, right-of-way proceedings were completed and in 1902 money was appropraited for dredging as far as the wharves of Ballard. Because of the opposition of Semple's group, the proviso was included that this should not be construed as adoption of a project for canal construction. Some excavating had been done toward Lake Union, borings were taken and the subject was reexamined to see whether such a route would be practicable for the largest commercial and naval vessels. The board reported in January, 1903 that it was entirely feasible, but at that time not advisable because the demands of commerce did not justify the expense.

Some months earlier Semple had gone to Washington and blocked another appropriation to continue work on the canal beyond Salmon Bay.

However the following autumn nature took a hand in furthering the project. In September water was higher than usual in Lake Union, a break occurred in the earth dam at the outlet and a river gushed out through the normally shallow bed of Ross Creek and in the next 36 hours did more to excavate the desired channel than years of talking had accomplished. The gates of the portage canal were closed and Lake Union drained down to within a foot or two of high water level in Puget Sound.

Some residents were gleeful and thought the break should not be repaired, but sawmill men on Lake Union were loudly clamoring to have the dam closed as quickly as possible because they had to cease operations until they could get their logs into the mills. A piledriver was soon at work and once more the water was rising in Lake Union.

Although the local district engineer's office submitted an estimate for building the canal to Lake Union, no action was taken. Once again a report was ordered and in 1906 Maj. Hiram M. Chittenden, who had been associated with many government projects in the East, was designated to make the investigation. Questions had arisen as to whether the proposed canal should have one or two locks. Some business interests advocated building a main lock at Fremont instead of nearer the Sound.

Major Chittenden was convinced that the most important piece of business before him was completion of the canal. He immediately traveled the entire length of the proposed route to Shilshole Bay and covered Lake Washington completely by boat.

Writing his first impressions of Seattle, Chittenden said, "It would not surprise me any to see here 500,000 people within ten years. Nowhere have I ever seen the earth torn up over an equal extent of country (the first regrade of Denny Hill was in progress) in the work of building up a new community. It is very crude, ugly and inconvenient now, but this is only a stage in the evolution of great things."

That July he wrote: "The Lake Washington Canal matter took a turn which was a great disappointment to me. I had hoped there might be an appropriation and that I might build this canal. But on account of adverse reports by the Department of Engineers, based as it seems to me on wholly misleading information, there was so little prospect of government aid that a (new) plan was adopted of doing the work with local capital and an Act of Congress was passed authorizing James A. Moore to build the canal."

Moore, who had worked as a contractor on the Denny Hill regrade, asked that King County contribute $500,000 to the canal cost. It was stipulated that the project must be completed within three years.

The plan received a setback when the State Supreme Court ruled against the legality of issuance of bonds by King County for this purpose.

Moore had proposed a wooden lock 600 feet long, 75 feet wide and 25 feet deep, whereas Chittenden advocated masonry and concrete construction. He completed in detail a workable plan for the entire canal and when he was finished with the report nothing more was needed than a congressional appropriation to activate it.

Matters dragged on. The decision for a timber lock was regretted and a masonry one was desired. Moore edged out and in 1907 assigned his rights to the Lake Washington Canal Association, which obtained an extension of time and began work at the portage. A new right-of-way was obtained there, reducing the curvature. But the project proved too much for local interests to handle and again appeals went to the federal government for aid.

That year Major Chittenden secured a congressional appropriation for another survey which would take the canal through University of Washington property instead of keeping it entirely inside of Harvey Pike's old Union City tract.

Meanwhile Ballard millmen saw the canal as a threat to their waterfront and organized to halt construction. They were too late. It was now moving slowly. The 1909 State Legislature appropriated $250,000 toward it from funds accumulated by the sales of shorelands. In 1910 King County voted a canal bond issue of $740,000 and on June 25, 1910 Congress finally authorized federal participation. In 1911 ground was broken for the locks.

Then commenced a five-and-a-half year construction period during which 4,000,000 cubic yards of dirt were dredged from the canal site and 230,000 yards of concrete were poured for the locks. They are second in size only to the Panama Canal locks in the United States. The large lock, 760 feet long and 80 feet in width, provides a channel 34 feet deep.

Before the locks were built Lake Washington's elevation fluctuated between 29 and 33 feet above mean lower low water in Puget Sound. Salmon Bay and Shilshole Bay were navigable at high tide, but practically dry at extreme low tide. Lake Union was regulated at about its present elevation, 21 feet. When the canal was completed Lake Washington was lowered to this level.

One of the problems not considered in the original plans was that salt water climbs into fresh bodies and there was danger of the lakes becoming salt. A special drain had to be introduced after a study of the situation was made. A salt water basin about 2,000 feet long and 250 feet wide is immediately above the large lock, and from the lower end of the basin is a discharge conduit and spillway dam. Sometimes the salt water has intruded enough to make Lake Union one-third as salty as Puget

Canal opening - The Roosevelt, Admiral Peary's ship in which he discovered the North Pole, led the marine pageant through Montlake Cut July 4, 1917 when the canal was formally opened. *Seattle Times photo from McDonald collection.*

Sound in seasons when many pleasure boats go through, but the salt water never has reached Lake Washington.

The distance from deep water in Puget Sound to deep water in Lake Washington is approximately eight miles. The total canal cost $5,000,000.

Opening of the waterway was a great event celebrated on July 4, 1917. A procession of 200 small boats was led by Admiral Peary's flagship, the *Roosevelt*. Hundreds of bouquets were thrown in the channel as the marine parade passed and a Boeing Model C airplane sputtered overhead. There was dancing that night in the streets of Fremont and fireworks were set off over Ballard.

Completion of the canal during the First World War enabled naval training ships to dock at the University of Washington, which became like a western Annapolis for the duration.

New Land on the Lakeshore

The change in the lake was gradual, occurring during the period between August 25 and October 21, 1916. One oldtimer recalled that for a year the level was raised and lowered. Persons with moorages had to move farther and farther out. Said the woman who had lived at Bryn Mawr, "The marsh was like a flower garden and my cabbages grew as

MIRACLE OF PROGRESS ON LAKE UNION

Lake Union "way back when" its industrial possibilities were totally undeveloped and few Seattle pioneers had visualized by 1890 how the area would look in 1937. The lower photo, from the collection of John Davis & Co., was taken forty-seven years ago; the upper view shows the lake as it appears now from the roof of the Ben Lomond Apartments. The $2,750,000 Aurora Bridge, built in 1933; the City Light Department plant in the foreground, and the Seattle Gas Company plant across the lake, all testify to the tremendous growth of the city and the opportunities for the investor with faith in the future of real estate, acquired either for industrial expansion or its income value. Seattle realtors are offering many downtown and outlying properties now that fit this formula.

Seattle Times article October 10, 1937

Laborers with shovels cut away the narrow strip of earth forming the cofferdam on the Lake Union side of the Montlake cut in August, 1916. *University of Washington Library*

big as buckets the first two years. Then suddenly everything grew up thickly with willows. We were sorry to see things changed. Lowering of the lake broke up our resort business."

A Kirkland resident who was living in Seattle when he was eight years old remembered one sunny day when a neighbor girl took him to see the water pouring through the Montlake cut. "We sat on the edge of the canal," he related, "and watched the muddy, turbulent water flowing through, much like the rapids in a river—cascading, not a smooth flow. I'll never forget the sight."

At Juanita and Kirkland the early docks had to be abandoned and the former community ceased to be a lake port. At Houghton the Anderson shipyard wharf was still usable, so the ferries came in there until new facilities were hastily constructed at the foot of Market Street.

In the Points country the three bays—Yarrow, Cozy Cove and Fairweather—were considerably shortened at their southern end and some landings were no longer usable. Dock pilings were left high and dry above the water. Houses stand today where formerly the lake was several feet deep.

The old gas works on Lake Union has been converted into a city park. *Photo by Greg Gilbert*

Mercer Slough ceased to be a lengthy waterway and steamboats could no longer go up to the sawmill at Wilburton. At the mouth another problem was created: snags were exposed and boats could not approach land on the south side. For some time residents all around the lake complained that they lacked communications because launches could no longer come in without hitting obstacles on the bottom. The passenger steamer *Triton* was snagged and sunk near the south end of Mercer Island.

The biggest change was in the land which appeared on the lakeshore side of railroad tracks and roads that formerly had been close to the water. Roughly 1896 acres were reclaimed. The greatest gain was 610 acres at Union Bay. At Mercer Slough, Juanita Bay and other indentations receding water left new expanses of swamp. Riviera Place on the west shore was new land. The University of Washington stadium, the Edmundson Pavilion and campus housing erected on the fill near Laurelhurst all stand where once was lake. This is also true of the Boeing plant at Renton, the airfield there, the park at Sand Point and the Shuffleton power station.

Lake Union lay largely undisturbed, its shorelands mostly in government title until a deficit occurred in financing the Alaska-Yukon-Pacific Exposition and the legislature authorized their sale. This smaller lake is shallow—only 40 feet in average depth—and it never became the wharfage site of large vessels, as had been envisaged before the canal. The bottom is a muddy jelly, often disturbed by land fills along the shore. Since 1906 a fifth of the lake has vanished because of such encroachments. This has alarmed concerned citizens, who would like to see limits set on fills and heavy building construction.

Though the canal brought Navy vessels into Lake Washington to the Naval Air Station, cargo ships for repairs or lay-ups at the Houghton shipyard, others to the mill and creosote works at Kennydale and log-towing boats to several booming grounds, there never was the great influx of large craft foreseen by early advocates of the waterway. In time the principal use was for pleasure boats and the fishing vessels that moored all the way from Shilshole Bay into Lake Union.

Thousands of small boats of every description pass through the locks on weekends and the place has become a major tourist attraction. Spectators in good weather enjoy watching the constant marine parade, as well as the salmon that go up through the fish ladder on the south side.

Sunday crowd - in the large locks *Greg Gilbert photo*

FOR A TASTE OF FRESH WATER

The Fremont drawbridge lifted high to permit passage of the picturesque sailing vessel Commodore through Lake Washington canal to anchorage in Lake Union. Today the famous vessel, one of the last sailing vessels to operate regularly in a trade route on the Pacific, lies at anchor opposite the Lake Union Dry Dock on Fairview near East Garfield St. The ship's future is indefinite. 2-14-35

VETERANS OF THE SEA FIND A HAVEN IN SEATTLE'S INLAND HARBOR: A SCENE ON LAKE UNION

A group of old-time sailing vessels at anchor, their forest of masts silhouetted against the evening sky. —*Times Photo*

A GALLANT SHIP MAKES ITS LAST LANDFALL NEAR SEATTLE AT EVENTIDE

Sun and sky are tinged a deeper red as greedy flames feast on one of the many old sailing ships which have been burned for their metals at Richmond Beach recently.

THE SEATTLE DAILY TIMES

FOR FREEDOM OF THE SEAS

Two ships of Seattle's idle fleet of windjammers, which have known the freedom of the seas, were saved today from being made prisoners in Lake Union by the new Aurora Street Bridge, now nearing completion. The vessels are the barks Moshulu and Monongahela, which have masts 190 feet high, while the central span of the bridge has a clearance of only 135 feet. The picture shows the Moshulu being towed through the small gap in the central span which soon will be bridged. The Monogahela followed. The vessels are being taken to Eagle Harbor. See Page 1 for news story. (Photo copyrighted by Kirwin.)

During the 1920's and 1930's Lake Union became a warehouse of sailing ships awaiting refurbishing or destruction. Scores of these majestic vessels were burned on the lake and at Richmond Beach for the scrap metal they contained. The above articles were published in the Seattle Times from 1929 thru 1935. *From the collection of O. M. Salisbury.*

Looking west up the ship canal with the Aurora Avenue and Fremont bridges in the foreground. *Photo by Greg Gilbert.*

NUTONE

The Opening Day parade. *Photo by Roy Scully*

Boating

Half a dozen or more boating clubs have headquarters on the two lakes, most venerable of which is the Seattle Yacht Club. It had formerly owned a club house on the Sound, but with the opening of the canal, the members saw advantages in moving to fresh water. Rough waves kicked up by steamers almost upset boats on the Sound, storms caused vessels to drag their moorings and oil dumped in the water was another disagreeable feature.

During the First World War, when the Emergency Fleet Corporation offered to purchase the old clubhouse as a training station for the merchant marine, search was begun for a new site on the canal.

The present clubhouse on Hamlin Street in Montlake was opened May 1, 1920 with considerable fanfare. The event set the pattern for an annual marine celebration known as Opening Day, always on the first Saturday of May. Then several thousand pleasure craft turn out for a procession through the Montlake cut and races on Lake Washington. Powerboats churn easily through the channel where once Indians had to portage their canoes across a neck of land from one lake to the other.

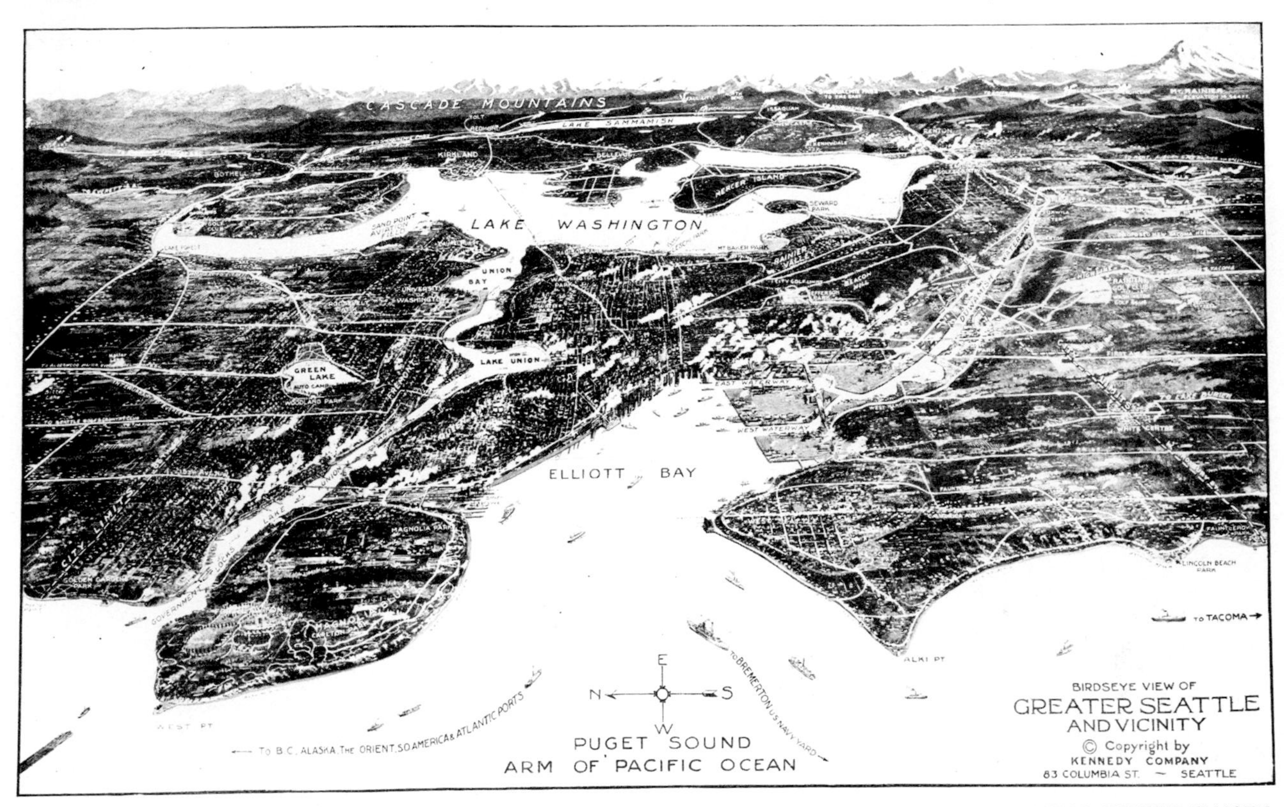

SEATTLE HAS ONE OF THE FINEST NATURAL HARBORS IN THE WORLD. COMPREHENSIVE VIEW OF SEATTLE HARBOR, SHOWING ELLIOTT BAY, DUWAMISH WATERWAY, LAKE WASHINGTON CANAL, LAKE UNION AND LAKE WASHINGTON. TOTAL APPROX. FRONTAGE, 200 MILES.

Old map showing this area's extensive waterways in 1929. *From collection of O. M. Salisbury.*

Opening Day is an occasion when boat owners from far and near participate. It is one of the great sights of Seattle.

Sailboating for small craft largely centers on Leschi, where the Corinthian Yacht Club has moorages. Any summer afternoon one may see sails in that vicinity and in winter the docks are a forest of masts where boats are hauled up out of the water. Several times during the season large sailboats race on the lake, running usually almost to the northern end.

Boating is a way of life around Lake Washington and a large percentage of families own at least an outboard motor and a skiff. If they do not live on the shore they patronize the nearest launching ramp. Water skiing is a common recreation.

Outboarders have their day once a year when races are staged for them on the Sammamish River. More than 100 craft may enter the events, witnessed by thousands of fans lining the banks.

Overshadowing all other types of racing is that for unlimited hydroplanes, scheduled annually in Lake Washington during Seafair, the first week of August.

Sometimes these races have had as their incentive a national trophy, the Gold Cup. The winning boat in this contest each year can take the race to its home water the following season. In 1950 a Seattle craft, Stanley S. Sayres' Slo-Mo IV, surprised eastern sports fans by capturing the cup at Detroit. The race came to Seattle the following year for the first time and a succession of winning boats kept it

Hydroplane races. *Photo by Greg Gilbert*

here continuously for several seasons. Until then the Gold Cup contests never had been held west of the Mississippi River since they were started in 1904. The annual winner carried away a $25,000 purse. After Seattle finally lost a race the Seafair trophy was set up locally.

Hydroplane racing brings crowds from other parts of the Pacific Northwest. The course lies south of the original Lake Washington Floating Bridge, west of Mercer Island and east of the hydroplane pits at Wetmore Slough. These were developed after the Mount Baker Park pit became too crowded for the purpose.

Pleasure boats tied up south of the hydroplane pits. *Photo by Greg Gilbert*

Yachts passing through the Lake Union section of the canal. *Photo by Greg Gilbert*

Lake Union in 1925 looking west to Queen Anne Hill. The vessels from left to right include The Ruby (foreground), Fulton (barge), Fort Laramie, Monitor, Thistle, Thomas P. Errich, Aurora, Anna M. Campbell. *Photo by O. M. Salisbury*

View of Seattle's skyline from Lake Union. Sailboats can be seen any day when there is a slight breeze. *Photo by Greg Gilbert.*

Scene looking across the lake from Magnuson Park, which was created from part of the Sand Point naval reservation. *Photo by Greg Gilbert*

Sand Point

Sand Point Naval Air Station came into existence after the lowering of the lake. During the First World War a group of aviators, visiting Seattle to promote a Liberty Bond drive, found that the only available landing place was Jefferson Park Golf Course.

The commandant of the Bremerton Naval Shipyard assigned a captain to work with a commission to look for a suitable Navy aviation field near the city. By motorboat and automobile he visited the lakes and found at Sand Point everything he was seeking. The commission purchased 219 acres there and ground was broken on June 19, 1920. The following year a strip 500 feet wide and 2,000 feet long was cleared.

At the urging of the Seattle Chamber of Commerce the county commissioners enlarged the field and it was used for testing 200 Boeing planes built for the government. A small sheet-iron hangar was the first building.

Pilots in early years took off from a dusty strip that was little more than a trail through woods. Rain turned the ground to mud and planes had to be mounted on pontoons and flown from the lake. Experiments were tried in sowing grass on the runway and this attracted so many ducks a sentry was posted to prevent damage in landing.

By 1924 these troubles were ironed out and the field received publicity as the starting point of the Army's first round-the-world flyers. That summer aircraft squadrons of the battle fleet established a tent camp and early in 1926 the Navy erected a temporary hangar for training planes. From then on the establishment grew to a base with as many as 550 officers and 2,450 men.

On July 1, 1970 the naval air station ceased to exist as such and became the Seattle Naval Support Activity, with the runway closed and about a third of the base shut down. Floor space was occupied largely by civilian employees, providing such services as Navy supply, billeting, administration of tenant activities on the base, processing of personnel returning to civilian life and operation of the naval district's correctional center. Courts martial in the Puget Sound area all convened there.

Much negotiation went into finding other uses for the base. It now has three owners, the Navy retaining the western 150 acres and the National Oceanic and Atmospheric Administration establishing a research center on the northern 150 acres. The remaining 195.6 acres were transferred to the city of Seattle for a park.

Near Sand Point was formerly another landmark in aviation history. Pan American World Airways initiated its Alaskan service in 1938 with amphibian planes departing from Mathews Beach. Flights from there were continued until March, 1941, when permission was granted by Canada for use of American land planes over British Columbia. In the beginning no adequate marine bases existed in the north and there was a scarcity of radio aids anywhere on the route. Only mail and express were carried in the exploratory years. Regular semiweekly commercial service by Sikorsky flying boats did not start until June, 1940; it had to be suspended that winter and was resumed again in spring. The planes flew directly out to sea from Mathews Beach.

The little seaplane base on Lake Washington was merely an interim operation until land planes out of Boeing Field could take over. All the proving work was done from Mathews Beach and the line between there and Juneau signified a great advancement for Alaskans, making it possible for them to reach New York in less than 30 hours instead of depending on boat service to Seattle, which consumed four days. It was considered a great feat when one could go to Juneau in seven hours, with a stop at Ketchikan.

Until Pan American launched its service from the base on the lake, Alaska had been as far away from the mainland United States as Europe.

The Kenmore Air Harbor is the largest seaplane base in the country. Begun in 1946, it is the only one to survive of many that started locally about the same time. Most seaplanes around Seattle are stored there and as many as 70 fly out of Kenmore. In addition charter service is maintained for sportsmen bound for remote lakes and for businessmen and mechanics wanting to reach towns, mills or ships off the regular air lanes.

Aerial view of Sand Point Air Base, which is now obsolete.
Photo by Greg Gilbert

Magnuson Park - Ramps for pulling small pleasure craft out of the water are essential when so many boat lovers live in the metropolitan district. *Photo by Greg Gilbert.*

Carkeek Park - This was the bell tower in 1918 in Carkeek Park, which once occupied the site of Mathews Beach. Morgan Carkeek, shown standing with his daughter, operated a brick plant at Pontiac, nearby. *Seattle Historical Society photo*

arkeek Park, Seattle

Sammamish River boating.

Mouth of the Sammamish River near Kenmore. *Photo by Greg Gilbert.*

Sammamish River

Army engineers explored the Sammamish River in 1912 in connection with plans for the ship canal and recommended as a most desirable improvement straightening and deepening the west end as far as Bothell "with a view to better navigation facilities."

Two boats then making regular trips to that place carried freight and passengers. It was anticipated after the lake was lowered the river would become swifter and unfit for navigation except at high stages. Bothell citizens protested in 1916 because it looked as though their stream was to become merely a drain. They owned a public wharf and reminded the government they had always had navigation facilities and now were to be deprived of them.

The Sammamish meandered a great deal and, though 17 miles in length, the distance from source to mouth was only 10 miles. Its flow was sluggish and the width varied from 50 to 150 feet. At flood seasons it inundated large areas of farm land.

Six months of the year logs floated down river, reaching a peak of about 12,000,000 feet in 1910 and declining after that as the surrounding country was cut over.

In steamboat days the little river towns had baseball teams and on Sundays it was a great thing to fill up a boat with about 140 passengers and go from Madison Park up the Sammamish to a ball game. The steamers had two decks and folding stacks to get them under the bridges. Neither vessel had a draft greater than four feet eight inches.

Straightening the river was long talked about, principally to relieve flood conditions. Some years ago it was adequately widened and deepened and the worst bends were removed. It is a good place now for outboards and several small marinas have been developed along the way.

Cedar River

To many persons living around Seattle, Cedar River means only one thing—a watershed. They are unaware that the 45-mile-long stream, Lake Washington's principal tributary, gained importance before the coming of white men. Indians discovered that Yakima Pass, near its headwaters, was the easiest walking route through the Cascade Range. Planes flying the air lane over Cedar River Valley today soar above the oldest path to Puget Sound that was followed by both red men and fur traders.

Cedar River always has been in a line of travel.

How the south end of the lake looks from the air. The mouth of the Cedar River can be seen to the left of the Boeing plant, Mercer Island is in the mid-center. *Photo by Greg Gilbert.*

Three railroads formerly were in the watershed and one is still there.

The upper valley was mostly government land when F.H. Whitworth, exploring for coal in 1881, suggested in a letter to the Seattle city council that here was a suitable spot for headworks and dams of the Water Department. The Cedar was the closest to the city of the high, snow-fed mountain streams and was best for a gravity system.

The Seattle fire influenced a vote in favor of this ambitious undertaking, but times were hard and money to carry it out was not available. In the interval that followed, the Seattle Power Co. was organized for the purpose of bringing Cedar River water to the city to wash out earth from Beacon Hill and excavate the proposed canal through it. The firm offered to sell some of its water to Seattle on a long-term contract.

The city engineer responded by laying out a counterplan and ordering construction of headworks on Cedar River at Landsburg and finally water from this stream reached Seattle in 1901. Soon afterward electric power was also generated with the help of a crib dam built farther upstream. Traces of the earliest power house can be seen at Cedar Falls.

In years of heavy snow and sudden thaws the crib dam withstood flood hazards, but in November, 1911 Cedar Lake filled nearly five feet above the wooden wall, the planks gave way and only the low cement portion of the dam remained.

Simultaneously with phoned warnings that a flood was sweeping down the valley toward Renton, Seattle's water pipes went dry and her power went off. The two catastrophic happenings originated at different places on the Cedar. The power intake pipeline broke half a mile below the dam and this put the power plant, six miles downstream, out of commission. At Landsburg a bridge carrying two large water pipes across the river washed out, creating a 150-foot gap in both.

Seattle went bathless for several days and persons with the temerity to hang out washings were reported as lawbreakers. Others were censured for profiteering by selling water. Hundreds stood in line to fill buckets and pitchers at private springs or dipped containers into the shrinking supply in reservoirs.

The days when Tobin Avenue in Renton was filled with a raging torrent were fresh in memory when the residents formed a commercial waterway district and taxed themselves for a portion of the funds needed to turn Cedar River through a new channel into Lake Washington and away from its natural course into Black River.

Prior to completion of the ship canal, steadily increasing demands for power caused Seattle to build a sturdier Cedar River dam with greater holding capacity a mile and a half below the old one in 1914. The city also increased its holding to protect the watershed and absorbed two little towns. It now owns 65,500 acres extending from Landsburg to the summit of the Cascades. Some private property remains in the watershed and a limited amount of logging is carried on.

The Cedar, though trapped in a lake above the dam, still has some characteristics of a rampaging Western Washington river with a normal quota of floating branches and trash, which have to be screened out. Turbines at the power plant run only when needed. Years ago, when so much water was not required by the city, the power station ran at a greater capacity.

The dam has another purpose, that of flood control. It assists in regulating the level of Lake Washington. Renton used to have annual rowboat races in the river, but they had to be discontinued because they depended upon the releasing from the dam of more than the customary amount of water.

Anywhere above the Water Department intake the pure liquid of the basin is hoarded. Some streams not so clear have been diverted into a sump and pass through a glacial moraine that filters them. In another area, where no filter bed exists, the brown water from Lake Walsh is turned into the river below the Landsburg dam.

The Cedar River watershed has two distinctions: it is probably the largest forested tract owned by any city in the United States and the power plant was the first publicly owned hydroelectric development in the country.

The Cedar may be a short river, but it has a long pedigree. Few other streams its size could match it in usefulness.

Through its lower course, northwest of Landsburg, the channel was from 1912 to 1957 maintained by the local commercial waterway district. When this was dissolved the city of Renton took over its function. Except for water supply control structures, the Cedar is still a free-flowing stream, although its final course is beside the Boeing plant, between it and the air field. It pours into the lake between a level strip that bridges it.

Of the 600 trillion gallons in Lake Washington 1,100 cubic feet enter per second, 90 percent from the Cedar and Sammamish Rivers.

As Seattle has grown, increasing demands have been made on the Cedar for water supply. In the late summer of 1958, for example, almost all of the flow had to be diverted to the city. Since then Seattle has added another source, the Tolt River, and this has reduced demands on the Cedar. The Army Corps of Engineers has investigated means for insuring against further decreases in the fresh water inflow into the lake and various methods of maintaining current levels.

Lake Regulation

Where factories once were advocated for the lakeshore, industrialization is now strongly opposed and even the long-time custom of storing logs behind booms has virtually ended. The only industrial zoning is at Renton, Houghton, Kenmore and Kennydale, which with the commercial area at Leschi comprises less than five per cent on the shoreline.

No lake in the world is so closely regulated. A spokesman in the operations department of the Army Corps of Engineers said, "Even within the narrow limits of raising and lowering the level we receive complaints because boats or boat houses rest on the bottom or companies can't tow gravel barges or boat-building firms cannot hold launchings. The complainers invariably insist that the level is lower than ever before."

When the locks were opened in 1917 Congress set the limits in which the lake should be kept at 20 to 22 feet above mean low tide in Puget Sound. The level is reduced in December to permit homeowners to repair bulkheads and work on docks. The build-up for summer levels continues to May 1. One half of the water used at the locks is for flushing the salt water back into the Sound. This is what pulls the level down in the warm months when a constant stream of boats goes through.

Property owners continue to crowd their premises out into the lake and some suffer damage during wind storms which have been known to raise three to four foot waves. Sixty-five per cent of the shore is privately owned and another half mile belongs to clubs. Regulations require buildings to be 20 feet back from the water, but owners have circumvented this by bulkheading out beyond the normal shoreline. Such changes, though ever so slight, are going on constantly and rock walls are pushing residential property a few feet at a time farther into the lake. Then there are persons complaining of high water, who build their homes during the low-level season, without taking into account the rising height of the lake late in the spring.

Where once broad lawns were characteristic of many properties along the shore, rising values have caused the lots to fill and any waterfront is now at a premium. Extremely little remains publicly owned* and there are all too few places where one can go and launch a small boat.

**Note:* Nineteen percent of the shoreline has public access.

Houseboats were once common on the Seattle side of the lake. This scene was taken south of the end of Pine Street by James P. Lee. (Note: There is no Pine Street in that area now.) *University of Washington Library*

Houseboats

A characteristic feature of the canal shores is the houseboats. These do not extend into Lake Washington, but they are to be seen around Lake Union, Portage Bay and toward Fishermen's Wharf. In the bootleg era houseboats earned an unsavory reputation, but they gained respectability prior to the Second World War, when their number reached 2,500. Many of the decrepit ones were condemned and cleared out and all were connected to the city sewer system, to eliminate one of the objections to their presence.

The number is not half what is used to be,* but the houses are of better quality, modernized inside and often occupied by families of professors and professional men. Moorages today are scarce and fairly expensive.

Houseboat owners have no lawns to mow, but they have other maintenance problems, such as replacing the logs underneath periodically so as to maintain balance and flotation. If the owners fancy pets, they can attract innumerable wild ducks that expect to be fed. It is something like living in the country without the disadvantages of being far from the city.

**Note:* Prior to World War II a colony of 50 houseboats moored off Leschi.

Houseboats on Lake Union. *Photo by Greg Gilbert*

The first Lake Washington Bridge. *Photo by Greg Gilbert*

The Bridge Era

When the increasing number of commuters to Seattle from the East Side caused someone to say, "Let's build a bridge," the mere suggestion precipitated a controversy lasting nearly two decades.

In fact, every time another bridge is mentioned today opposition factions again arise, sounding warnings about fencing in the lake between spans. The earlier arguments about the futility of trying to cross so deep a body of water are now disproved and outworn.

The battle of the first bridge was the most difficult, for it was based on a concept new to this part of the world. How the idea for a span that floated came about was told by its originator.

On a spring morning in 1920 Homer M. Hadley, a young engineer employed in the Seattle school architect's office, was shaving in his home in the south end of Seattle overlooking the lake when suddenly an idea struck him. He could see from his window some unsightly wooden hulls left over from the First World War. They were moored near Kennydale. For some reason Hadley associated them in his mind with concrete barges built by the Emergency Fleet Corporation in Philadelphia where he formerly had worked.

Why not, he speculated, construct hollow concrete barges shaped on top like a roadway and connect them end to end to form a floating bridge? Enthusiastically he drew a cross section, providing each barge with three watertight compartments.

"I was utterly inexperienced," Hadley reminisced. "I thought bankers were the persons to whom one proposed financing toll bridges. I talked to one Seattle capitalist but he thought my idea pretty wild and looked on me as a screwball. Like most persons, he thought concrete ships or barges ultimately would become waterlogged and sink."

Private firms regarded any type of bridge to Mercer Island a greater investment than the small amount of traffic warranted. However, by 1922 it became desirable to shorten the North Bend-Seattle section of the highway to Eastern Washington. On the strength of this a group of Mercer Island residents proposed subscribing a fund to purchase 15 of the Shipping Board's surplus wooden vessels for $100 apiece and string them out to form a pontoon bridge between Seward Park and the island.

The old wooden span over the East Channel south of Bellevue was Mercer Islanders' only direct communication with the mainland. It was a 23-mile trip to Seattle over that route and around the south end of the lake. What commuters there were patronized the boats from Leschi and Rainier Beaches, particularly the motor launch *Dawn*, which made leisurely trips along the west side of the island, stopping at private docks. She was a 75 ton craft built by Anderson at Houghton in 1915.

King County was low on funds and the commissioners refused to sanction the pontoon proposal because, even though the islanders supplied the makeshift bridge, it would involve the expense of building and maintaining approach roads.

Bridge talk ended for the time being, but Hadley never gave up his theory about the utilitarian soundness of concrete barges. He had studied government surveys and heard arguments about the great depth of Lake Washington and the thick layer of soft mud on its bottom. Not content merely to suggest a radically new type of structure, he set out to find a suitable location for it.

On a Saturday afternoon he rode to Madison Park and walked for several miles along the ridge to the south, seeking the narrowest place for a traffic tunnel. At Atlantic Street he saw that the Mount Baker ridge dropped steeply on the western side and the Smith Tower appeared in a direct line at no great distance.

"I felt like Balboa when I discovered this place," Hadley said. "I was aware that the site of any future bridge would be an important factor in negotiations because of the high cost of constructing an approach. The spot I found is over the present tunnel, which is exactly 1,445 feet long. To have bored it a few hundred feet away on either side would have involved much greater expense."

Soon after his discovery Hadley became regional structural engineer for the Portland Cement Association.

"From then on, whenever I mentioned my idea," he recalled, "someone would express fear that it was part of a nefarious plot of the cement companies to desecrate the lake for profit."

In the next few years toll-bridge proposals continued to simmer, with the suggestion of wooden pontoons with concrete piers for anchors gaining support. This was in spite of a Seattle Times editorial that spoke scathingly of "hundreds of tossing, heaving pontoons" and "hideous barges which properly belong to military maneuvers" marring the lake's beauty and forming a barrier to water sports.

In November, 1928 the islanders, determined to get a span no matter where it was built or by whom, sent committees to appeal to the East Side communities to join the "Build-the-Bridge-Now" campaign.

That year the Puget Sound Bridge & Dredging Co. drew plans for a $1,000,000 toll bridge from Seward Park to a point on the southern part of Mercer Island, the narrowest spot along the west side of the lake. It would have 14 concrete piers, a 175-foot draw span, a 24-foot roadway and a single five-foot sidewalk for pedestrians. But it involved a 1,700-foot earth fill across Seward Park. Seattle's corporation counsel ruled that no franchise for a bridge with an approach through the park legally could be granted.

Another approach south of the park and entailing a longer fill like a railroad embankment was substituted, but the city council voted to table the bridge plans indefinitely. At some time during these negotiations the Puget Sound Bridge & Dredging Co. went to the extent of sending an engineer to Turkey to study the steel pontoon bridge across the Golden Horn in Istanbul.

Late in August, 1931 the Seattle city council appointed a committee to hold a public hearing on four applications for a franchise. Two groups proposed routes from Madison Park to the platted townsite of Muskingum (west of Clyde Hill). Another was the Seward Park plan and the last was Hadley's plan. He had found backers for a route from a point south of Leschi Park to East Seattle, with a second bridge from Roanoke to Medina across the East Channel.

An immediate protest was entered in behalf of the Navy against any bridge which might jeopardize the seaplane approach to Sand Point. Pontoon bridges were declared unsightly and impractical and The Seattle Times branded them as "unthinkable."

This left the Seward Park proposal for a high span, with a jack-knife draw, the most favored. Somewhere in this period there had been a plan for a $12,000,000 tube under the lake, but this was quickly abandoned as too costly.

In the next several years the style of the bridge changed and, although a franchise granted to the Seattle Toll Bridge Co. was extended, the firm was unable to finance the resulting plan. The bridge had grown to three lanes and 3,387 feet in length, including approaches. The county next tried to secure a federal grant against matching funds, plus a Public Works Administration loan so as to go ahead with the Seward Park project.

This was the program early in 1937, just before the Washington Toll Bridge Authority was created by the Legislature. When Hadley learned that the new board would insist upon making its own survey of possible locations, he called on Lacey V. Murrow, director of the State Department of Highways, and said he already had found the most direct and inexpensive site.

Murrow was receptive to Hadley's information and wanted to learn more. He proposed borrowing Hadley from the cement association, but in the end the fight over the bridge became so hot there was no chance of using anyone representing industry as a consultant. When rumors said Murrow favored Hadley's suggestion the Mount Baker and Seward Park community clubs launched a fight against ungainly pontoons, calling them "financial folly, an unnecessary tax burden and a desecration of the lake."

Murrow's engineers meanwhile examined the other routes and concluded that Hadley's was the

Mercer Island end of the bridge. *Photo by Greg Gilbert*

most practical. Opponents tried to have the plan for a 3,000 foot concrete pontoon bridge from Dearborn Street to the north end of Mercer Island blocked by the Secretary of the Interior.

"The scows will sink from sight in five years and Seattle will be the laughing stock of the nation," was the dire prediction.

Murrow stuck with the idea with a singleness of purpose and formed a consulting board for the bridge authority composed of prominent experts from other parts of the Pacific Coast. Community clubs went on actively fighting the plan. Climaxing the years of strife with a final dash of melodrama, the Public Works Authority in Washington D.C. in June, 1938, by error granted $1,550,000 for construction of the Seward Park bridge, then virtually a dead issue.

Murrow conceived his structure as part of a huge development. Taking his board of experts up in a plane, he outlined his plan for feeder highways and a tunnel under the Mount Baker district. He said the scheme would finance itself, that bond companies would see the bridge as a sound propositition and that tolls would pay off the indebtedness. He conducted a traffic survey to estimate the potential number of users as a basis for fixing toll charges.

Ground was broken for the bridge on December 17, 1938 and the first automobile went over it on June 5, 1940. The bridge officially opened July 2, the largest concrete-pontoon structure of its kind in the world. Not only was it an engineering marvel (it had the first shuttle pontoon in existence) but it shortened the Sunset Highway by 14 miles and approximately one hour's running time. Total cost of the six-and-a-half mile road project and its accompanying improvements was $8,854,000, part of it paid by a Public Works Administration grant and part by a $5,500,000 bond issue. It proved a sound financial investment and paid off its indebtedness ahead of schedule, becoming toll free in July, 1949.

As for Hadley's part in the scheme, only the theory and the location conformed with his proposal. His pontoons would have had another shape and his draw would not have bulged as the present one does. He went on to build other bridges in other places, but never had the pleasure of building one on pontoons, the wild idea he had fought for.

Evergreen Point Bridge at sunset. *Photo by Greg Gilbert*

The Second Bridge

Talk of a second bridge began in 1949, followed by much milling around where to put it and what type to build. The population of the East Side had increased enormously and soon predictions were being made that the metropolitan area within a few more than a score of years would reach out and be fairly solidly built up as far as the east shore of Lake Sammamish. Another direct means of reaching the city had to be provided, as traffic jams on the Lake Washington Bridge were increasingly frequent.

So many objections were raised to proposed sites for another bridge that several years were lost in litigation and re-surveys. Eventually in August, 1960 the Evergreen Point span was commenced, a more ambitious project than the earlier one. Again pontoons were employed, but this time no curved section at the draw. In the process of opening the bridge to ship traffic the lift spans are raised seven feet two inches to allow movable pontoons to retract underneath them.

First estimates of the cost of the second bridge were $9,500,000, but by the time of completion in August, 1963 the total cost, with highway interchanges had reached $34,000,000. The length of the project from its connection with the U.S. 5 freeway to 104th Avenue N.E. at the head of Yarrow Bay is 5.93 miles. The route crosses a viaduct over the end of Portage Bay, threads its way through the Union Bay marsh and across Foster Island. Its floating portion is 1.42 miles in length and consists of 18 standard and 15 special sections, including four fender pontoons. It is held in place by 62 anchors. Continual inspection and maintenance are necessary because of its exposed location.

Like the first bridge, it was required to pay for itself with tolls. Heavy use made it quickly self-supporting and it liquidated its indebtedness in June, 1979. Traffic on it is doubling every three years and the time is foreseen when the span will reach capacity.

Aside from utilitarian considerations the bridge is outstanding for its view in both directions on a clear day.

At its western side two fountains were placed in the lake, controlled by a time-clock and operated from 7 a.m. until midnight. When winds exceeded 15 to 20 miles an hour an automatic device shut them off so that the spray would not drift on the roadway. In freezing weather the fountains were turned off manually and drained.

A third Lake Washington bridge already is on the drawing boards. This one will be parallel to the Mercer Island bridge in order to double the use.

Engineers have recommended a fourth floating bridge, and possibly a fifth bridge.

Wild ducks ride out a stormy day near the east end of the Evergreen Point Bridge. *Photo by Greg Gilbert.*

Meanwhile a freeway east of the lake (Highway 405) was constructed to carry traffic direct from Snohomish and Woodinville south through Bellevue and Renton, connecting with U.S. 5 at Tukwila. Distances that formerly required a day to cover are reduced to half an hour's running time with an automobile. No place near the lake any more is far from Seattle.

How the East Side Grew

What has happened to the towns around the lake as the result of bridges and highways? Before construction of the first span Mercer Island's population did not exceed 500 permanent families, grouped on the northwestern part at East Seattle and Roanoke and scattered along the remainder of the 13 miles of shoreline.

Today Mercer Island is a city of 18,500, with a large shopping center and ample public utilities. It has become a dormitory suburb, where in 15 minutes driving time from his Seattle office, the resident finds himself in a country-like atmosphere.

Kirkland has grown in population to 14,266 and Juanita, to the north of it, has several times threatened to incorporate.

A conspicuous development at Kirkland is the number of shore apartment houses on land pumped in from the lake bottom or on piers out over the water.

Greater Bellevue, comprising the Bellevue School District, takes in the incorporated communities of Clyde Hill, Yarrow and Hunts Points, Medina, Beaux Arts and the unincorporated environs extending to Lake Sammamish and including such sizable areas as Lake Hills. The population in 1974 was 82,700.* The area covered is approximately 37 square miles and embraces 22 shopping centers, Bellevue Shopping Square and Crossroads. Among buildings is the 13-story Bellevue Business Center, tallest in town, and numerous corporate headquarters and several large motels.

Already the municipality has outgrown its City Hall, new in 1964 and a second structure is now in use. Bellevue has a community college and four high schools. A planned city, it has wide business streets, with provisions for off-street parking. Utility wires have gone underground.

Within Greater Bellevue are eight woodland parks and four swimming beaches. While single-family houses predominate, many distinctive suburban-type apartment houses have gone up.

Bellevue has come a long way since its skid roads and berry fields. Instead of holding rural strawberry festivals on school grounds, it is now the scene

Evergreen Point Bridge covered with spray. *Photo by Greg Gilbert*

Photo by Roy Scully

of the sophisticated Pacific Northwest Arts and Crafts Fair, which the last weekend in July sprawls over the central shopping square. Instead of being home port to whalers, its bays are filled with pleasure-boat moorages.

Some years ago Bellevue was designated an All American City. It has been trying to outstrip itself ever since.

**Note:* The 1977 population figure for Bellevue alone was 68,000.

Industries

Industrialization has been confined almost exclusively to the south end of the lake. Kennydale has three large installations, a factory for pre-fab houses, a sawmill and a piling company.

Next is the Shuffleton Steam Plant of the Puget Sound Power & Light Co., where standby power is generated up to 85,800 kilowatts. For several years steam from this power plant was used by the Boeing Co. in the testing of ram jet engines and the eerie sounds from the wind tunnel could be heard for miles. It also assisted the Seattle plants with research work on missiles. Because such types of research now are conducted at other, more remote sites, use of the Shuffleton laboratory by Boeing ended about the middle of 1965.

The Boeing Co. erected its Renton factory in 1941 and moved in the following year. The location on the waterfront at the mouth of the Cedar River was part swamp, part a plant nursery and partly occupied by a sawmill. Tremendous quantities of fill were required both for the factory and the air field. Earth was pumped by an offshore dredge from the bottom of the lake. The fill had to be allowed to settle before the 5,000-foot runway and taxiways were graded and paved.

Concrete ramps were constructed at the edge of the lake to accommodate a two-engine flying boat, a Navy patrol bomber, for which the plant originally was planned. The seaplane base northwest of the present runways was where Wiley Post and Will Rogers had their floatplane modified before their tragic flight to Alaska.

The Renton Division several years after the Second World War became the Transport Division, which in turn evolved into the Commercial Airplane Division. It was the birthplace of the XC-97 piston-engine Air Force transport and the Dash 80, the prototype for all members of Boeing's jet transport family, as well as for most of the earlier propeller-type EC-97 tanker-transports.

The Renton branch more recently produced the four-engine 707s and three-engine 727s. It also turned out many four-engine 720s.

When the plant opened it consisted of a 95 acre site with a covered floor totalling 2,300,000 square feet. By November, 1968 this had grown to 209 acres with 6,529,463 square feet of covered working areas.

Before leaving the Boeing Co., it should be said that another structure on the lake played a part in the firm's development. The oddly shaped canoe house on the University of Washington campus during the First World War was where groups of 30 Naval trainees built and maintained some of the firm's first planes made from spruce, wire and canvas. The project was started by Captain Miller Freeman, who set up an aviation school on the campus and, not having a plane to work with, contacted William E. Boeing, a wealthy lumberman's son, who was experimenting with flying machines. Boeing accepted the officer's proposition, supplied materials, taught classes and graduated 180 men, equipped not only to fly but to build and maintain aircraft. They proved a valuable contribution to America's part in the war.

Much older than the Boeing plant at Renton is the nearby Pacific Car and Foundry Co., which has been there since 1908 on an 88-acre site. In busy years its employment roll has reached 2,400. The Renton division is America's largest producer of sophisticated railroad refrigerator cars. It builds winches and hoists for logging and industrial uses, military transport and combat vehicles, steel and aluminum light poles, propellers, hose and fittings.

Another sizeable industrial plant is the former Gladding McBean Co., now INTERPACE, makers of clay products. Part of the clay is obtained at Renton and some is brought from a distance to be converted into building brick, pipes and construction materials.

Renton has shed completely its coal-town identity and is a community of 24,800 oriented to modern industries. Gone from the Cedar River Valley are Indians and mines; in their place are mobile-home courts, golf courses and recreation centers. To the southwest of the city is Longacres race track and, farther away, amid a network of freeway approaches, are the South Center shopping complex and the Tukwila industrial park.

At the north end of the lake Kenmore is the only area zoned for industries. Gravel and cement companies and several others are there, including the Pioneer Towing Co., which during Alaska pipe line construction loaded numerous large barges of material to start their journey north.

Defeating the Demon

While man has driven back the wildlife and brought many alterations to the lake shore, not all of his activities have been detrimental. He won a victory over the threat of pollution.

Warnings of this went back to Seattle's early search for a water supply. By 1922 the city dis-

The Boeing Company's Renton plant looks toward Lake Washington. The mouth of Cedar River is located between the buildings and the Renton Municipal Airport. *Photo courtesy the Boeing Commercial Airplane Co.*

Seward Park Ducks Facing Food Crisis

Fund Sought to Purchase Six More Tons of Grain to Tide Birds Over Winter Here

P-I 1/5/39

By Ken McLeod

Lake Washington's big colony of waterfowl, consisting of thousands of mallards, sprigs, butterballs, blue bills, coots and a few geese, which congregate annually during the winter months at Seward Park for its daily rations of corn and wheat, has sent out its warning call that the granary is running low.

A supply of grain for only two more weeks remains to feed the hungry flocks of waterfowl, which will remain in the vicinity until the latter part of March, or until there is no longer any threat of cold weather.

The late D. E. Frederick established the feeding grounds near Seward Park years ago, but in the fall of 1937 when Dr. Brien T. King announced that no provision had been made for the winter of 1937-38, big hearted lovers of the wild ducks rallied to the call for help.

Sufficient money was subscribed to the fund to feed the ducks throughout last winter and enough remaining to purchase six additional tons of grain which has been fed from early in October to the present time.

MAN TO FEED 'EM

The Seattle Park Department, in cooperation with Dr. King's efforts to raise the money, has provided a man to feed the birds daily. The park department has informed THE POST-INTELLIGENCER that approximately six more tons of grain will be required to carry the load through this winter.

That means, that if the ducks do not go hungry during the next two and one-half months, somebody will have to dig up approximately $175 with which to buy the estimated amount of feed.

Because of the drive for membership in the Ducks Unlimited movement, Dr. King has been hesitant about bringing the subject to light. But those ducks out there at Seward Park are not a bit backward about putting up a loud "quack" over their dwindling grain supply, and the noise they are now making is nothing to what it will be when the grain buckets are empty.

NEED CONTRIBUTIONS

Who has a dollar, or a five, or a ten to throw in the pot so that those Seward Park ducks will have a happy New Year?

It's a cause that few can find to argue against. It keeps the ducks in this locality to raise more broods of native birds and it provides a great attraction for nature lovers who want their ducks to look at, and not to shoot.

That's your cue, Mr. Duckhunter and Mr. Nature Lover—send in your contributions for the Seward Park Duck Fund to Dr. Brien T. King, Medical-Dental Building, Seattle—and Dr. King will pay for the feed the park department orders so your ducks won't go hungry.

They Must Be Fed

DR. BRIEN KING is one of the game bird enthusiasts who is pressing a campaign to secure funds to feed Lake Washington's native ducks this winter at Seward Park.

Seattle Post Intelligencer January 5, 1939

charged sewage into the lake from 33 outfalls, but four years later interceptors were built and in another 10 years the water was clearer than it had been in a long time.

Then in 1942 the first of a series of ten suburban sewage treatment plants was constructed and Lake Washington went into a second period of enrichment. Parts of it became dangerous for swimmers and at the Houghton shipyard there was sickness among workers from drinking polluted lake water.

Several types of algae always had been in the lake, but early in the 1940's the upper portion developed something zoologists nicknamed the "demon." This was the blue-green *Oscillatoria rubescens*, which took the form of floating patches of scum and slimy masses piled on gravel beaches. By 1955 this was becoming thoroughly discouraging to swimmers. The algae multiplied, fertilized by the enriching preparations spread on lakeshore lawns and carried off by sprinkling systems. There was also the seepage from septic tanks, and the detergents that went out in traps from kitchen sinks and laundry equipment.

In 40 years the amount of phosphorous draining into the lake had tripled and phosphorous made the algae thrive.

The Cedar River and to a lesser extent the Sammamish had been the chief natural sources of this chemical. Before the mountains were logged this element was held back by the soil, but in recent years it was carried away with the rains. Often fertilizer ran off with it from cultivated ground. The once-clear lake became somewhat like pea soup.

Much of the change was due to mass movements of population to the suburbs after the Second World War. The blue-green algae became a warning signal and studies were made under the direction of Dr. W.T. Edmondson of the University of Washington. In 1957 zoologists were alarmed to find the water at the bottom lacking in oxygen. When this happens continuously, slime forms on the bottom of a lake, the water smells and gas bubbles up from it.

That was the year the Metro system sewage program began, independent systems were brought to an end and gradually new trunk sewers reached out to carry the effluent to a disposal plant on Puget Sound.

Lake conditions have improved greatly and this is one of the rare ecology success stories where history was reversed.

Wildlife

There is one important reason why hunting is not allowed around Lake Washington. It is a game preserve and has been one for nearly 70 years. Before that the east side of the lake was considered open country for sportsmen and gradually as farming and logging made access easier for hunters there was a diminution in the wildlife.

As the year of the Alaska Yukon Pacific Exposition approached a consciousness of the value of conservation developed in some quarters. Talk of creating a game preserve was heard and finally a bill was approved in the State Legislature on March 6, 1909, making it unlawful to fire a gun, kill, shoot, trap, snare or in any manner destroy or maim wild birds at any season of the year upon the lake or within a mile of it. Fines or jail sentences could be imposed as a penalty.

Not everyone took the law seriously at first. A man on the north shore encountered a deer in his back yard, shot it and enjoyed venison dinners. He made the mistake of boasting about this piece of luck and word reached the authorities. The sheriff paid him a visit and placed him under arrest.

As a consequence of the law a multitude of game birds is often to be seen at favorite feeding places. The commonest are mallard ducks which become so tame, if they stay the year around, that they will feed within a foot or two of persons offering bread or grain. Geese arrive in sizable flocks during their migrations and one family at Pleasure Point counted 52 Canadian honkers feeding on the lawn. Even swans stray off their flyways and have been known to drop in.

Seldom does a lakeshore dweller look out of his windows without seeing mallards, coots (mud hens) or widgeon feeding. Some mornings a stray grebe or loon will be out on the water with them. Often there are ducks of unknown varieties, the result of interbreeding.

Scores of species of birds frequent the lakeshore and any censustaker for the Audubon Society has a rewarding task. A striking resident is the Steller's jay; another is the great blue heron. Humming birds are there in summer and the cattail swamps abound in tule wrens. Infinite variety prevails, for birds like the lakeshore as much as human beings do.

Of wildlife some remain in the swamps—beaver, muskrat, an occassional mink—but the otter and others have retreated to uninhabited places up the Sammamish. Some years ago nutria, escaped from captivity at a fur farm, were often seen, but these, too, seem to have left the large lake for the hinterlands.

On the East Side raccoons are common in wild places, deer stray down to civilization and in a hungry season bear and coyotes have been reported. At Issaquah it is only a step into the wild habitat of these animals.

Union Bay is still a place in which to find the

Ducks among the tules south of Seward Park. *Photo by Greg Gilbert*

unusual; for example, big freshwater clams, which once were common in places where water flowed from outlet streams. They were abundant in the Sammamish River until the Army Engineers dredged and straightened it. In soft sediments in the deep part of the lake scientists find tiny fingernail clams.

Crayfish are another disappearing item. Some are still in the Sammamish River, but those formerly in the ship canal are gone. Two species of frogs occur in fair numbers in Union Bay.

Fish

What really abounds is fish. Strangely, despite encroachments of civilization, Lake Washington has the potential of being one of the best bodies of water in the state for fishing. It contains plenty of algae, the natural food for fish, and an abundance of small varieties for the carnivorous larger ones to feed on. The many little bays are natural rearing areas and the variety of inlets afford places where small fry can seek cover.

Sports fishing can be done, but anyone over the age of 16 must have a license. Over the age of 70 he can obtain it for free.

The first scientific work on the lake was done for the United States Fish Commission in 1898, when investigators reported finding trout, squawfish, suckers, black bass, yellow perch and sockeye salmon, which they called redfish.

This list still applies, but with the addition of many others: bluegill, kokanee (landlocked silver trout), chubs, croppies, catfish, carp, cutthroat trout, steelhead and Japanese green tinch, a heritage of the 1909 Alaska Yukon Pacific Exposition. The last were dumped in the lake when no other use could be found for them after the Japanese closed their exhibit at the fair. The fish took kindly to the new surroundings and generations of them have bred. Mystifying to some persons are the catfish young, which appear occasionally in groups of hundreds, swimming like a dark cloud in the water.

Salmon go up the lake into the Sammamish River, Lake Sammamish and Issaquah Creek, where a salmon hatchery is maintained by the state.

How a sportsman's basket used to look after a few hours near the Cedar River. *From a Seattle Chamber of Commerce booklet.*

This explains to a certain extent the salmon seen mounting the fish ladder at the locks. Some return to the School of Fisheries ponds at the University of Washington. Others go to a few of the 464 streams draining into the basin, though most of these have succumbed to the encroachments of urban sprawl and have ceased to offer an invitation to the salmon. Cohoes, or silvers, are known to travel far up, leaving their eggs in drainage ditches beside roads and in rivulets that disappear in summer. Some communities are endeavoring to check the decline in spawning grounds, clearing debris from the mouths of streams and replanting them with young fish.

Beside sockeyes and silvers a few kings run into the lake. Since 1935, sockeyes have been restored artificially to Cedar River, which also is well known to sportsmen for its steelhead trout. About 90 percent of the sockeyes in the lake are spawned there, the run having increased slowly until 1971 it reached 553,000 and the question arose about harvesting it. This species does not normally take to sports lures and no one wanted commercial fleets in Lake Washington with gill nets and purse seines. Finally it was agreed to permit seiners nearby in the Sound and open the south end of the lake to Muckleshoot Indian fishermen.

Increase in all fish has been partially due to the clearing of the lake. The sockeyes begin gouging spawning beds in gravel in late September and the season continues until December. The parent fish die and the young remain in the lake a year, growing to about five and a half inches in length, then they migrate to sea between April and June, staying away two years. Only about one percent of those that leave return to spawn. Because so many head for Cedar River the Seattle Water Department is compelled to maintain minimum flows there. But besides the need to keep water on the spawning grounds a certain flow is required for operation of the locks, maintaining the level of the lakes and permitting flushing back of salt water from the locks.

Seattle is the only place in the world that has a salmon run of such great proportions passing through the heart of a city. More than a million dollars worth in a good year head for Cedar River. With their bright red flesh, they are a top canning variety and the fish from Lake Washington are said to be especially robust.

The Weather

Something deserves to be said of the weather on the lake, mild enough more than half of the year to permit water skiing.

Wind storms sometimes churn the surface into white caps and build up waves in a northerly direction that do damage to private docks, especially if floating logs are on the loose, acting as battering rams.

The water in winter is often warmer than the surroundings. Residents are not surprised on chilly mornings to find a large pink cloud hovering over the water and wisps of steamy vapor rising to it from the surface.

The only time ice was on the water in recent years was in February, 1950, when a little extended out from Lake Forest Park, Kenmore and Inglewood. Long ago the forests held the snow longer, temperatures were colder and smaller Lake Union froze over. Witness to this is a newspaper story of February, 1875, telling of the coal company cutting a channel 50 feet wide and three miles long acress the lake to allow continuous transportation of the fuel from the portage to Seattle. The ice was from eight to ten inches thick at that time.

In the more than a century since white men first penetrated the lake country it has changed mightily. The loggers are gone and subdivisions have taken the place of virgin forests. The railraod that rimmed its northwestern shore has been pulled up and a hiking-biking trail has taken its place. With cars speeding along its surrounding highways no one would think of reviving a much-touted event of the 1920's, a hiking race completely around the lake. The last ferry ceased operating in the summer of 1950, the private amusement parks have been superseded by city and county parks. Open spaces have filled up and population has spread completely around the shores.

But the greatest space of all, Lake Washington, remains its serene self, fringed with madrona, dogwood, fir and cottonwood trees, dotted with boats and flanked by mountains. It is still a place of awe-inspiring views, summer nights that remind one of the tropics, magnificent sunsets, days when the peak of Mount Rainier rises like Fujiyama over the south shore. On other days the mountain summit, detached from its base, appears floating above a mass of clouds. Then there are days when winds of gale velocity churn the water and it splashes in foam against bulkheads, sending showers high in the air.

Winter comes and the fragile branches of deciduous trees frame frosty views of the gleaming water. Unforgettable is Christmas week, when lighted pleasure boats parade, stopping before blazing bonfires and carols ring out on the still nights. This is today a local tradition, as much so as when the old excursion boats circled the lake and visitors were told there was no other place like it.

Seward Park in winter. *Photo by Greg Gilbert*

The Christmas Ship - always leads a holiday parade on the lake *Greg Gilbert photo*

Dogwoods create beauty spots on the lake shore. *Photo by Greg Gilbert*

BIBLIOGRAPHY

Data sheet and interviews from the U.S. Engineers Office
J.E. Whitworth diary, University of Washington Library
U.S. Coast and Geodetic Survey reports
Map of Union City, 1890, Museum of History and Industry
Collection of clippings from Pan American World Airways
Recollections of lake steamers from Puget Sound Maritime Historical Society members
Communications from Prof. W.T. Edmondson
Seattle Illustrated (Ch. of Com. publication), 1890
Boeing Co. History of Renton plant
Bellevue Chamber of Commerce
Renton Chamber of Commerce
Mrs. Colman's diaries
Early files of the Intelligencer
Pacific Northwest Quarterly July, 1962 and October, 1962
Chittenden family folder on ship canal
Washington Title Co. records
Bagley's History of King County
Snowden's History of Washington
Grant's History of Seattle
Clippings from three newspapers
Mainly I relied on personal interviews with pioneers and letters from their families, received while I prepared a Seattle Times series running October 2, 1955 through February 26, 1956, also numerous articles I wrote at other times, based on pioneer research and interviews.

The west end of the two bridges with Mount Rainier and the Cascades for a background. *Photo by Roy Scully.*

Index